Women of the Civil War

Titles in the Women in History series include:

Women of the American Revolution
Women of Ancient Rome
Women of the Middle Ages
Women of the 1960s

Women of the Civil War

Stephen Currie

LUCENT
BOOKS®

THOMSON
────✦────
GALE

San Diego • Detroit • New York • San   Waterville, Maine • London • Munich

On cover: A nurse cares for wounded Union soldiers during the Civil War.

LIBRARY OF CONGRESS CATALOGING-IN-PUBLICATION DATA

Currie, Stephen, 1960–
    Women of the Civil War / by Stephen Currie.
        p. cm. — (Women in history series)
Summary: Explores the inmpact of the Civil War on women's lives, as well as the
many roles played by women on and off of the battlefields.
Includes bibliographical references and index.
    ISBN 1-59018-170-0 (hardback : alk. paper)
    1. United States—History—Civil War, 1861–1865—Women—Juvenile literature.
[1. United States—History—Civil War, 1861–1865—Women. 2. Women—History—
19th century. 3. United States—History—Civil War, 1861–1865—African
Americans.] I, Title. II. Series.
    E628 .C87 2003
    973.7'082—dc21
                                                                    2002004108

Printed in the United States of America

Contents

Foreword

The story of the past as told in traditional historical writings all too often leaves the impression that if men are not the only actors in the narrative, they are assuredly the main characters. With a few notable exceptions, males were the political, military, and economic leaders in virtually every culture throughout recorded time. Since traditional historical scholarship focuses on the public arenas of government, foreign relations, and commerce, the actions and ideas of men—or at least of powerful men—are naturally at the center of conventional accounts of the past.

In the last several decades, however, many historians have abandoned their predecessors' emphasis on "great men" to explore the past "from the bottom up," a phenomenon that has had important consequences for the study of women's history. These social historians, as they are known, focus on the day-to-day experiences of the "silent majority"—those people typically omitted from conventional scholarship because they held relatively little political or economic sway within their societies. In the new social history, members of ethnic and racial minorities, factory workers, peasants, slaves, children, and women are no longer relegated to the background but are placed at the very heart of the narrative.

Around the same time social historians began broadening their research to include women and other previously neglected elements of society, the feminist movement of the late 1960s and 1970s was also bringing unprecedented attention to the female heritage. Feminists hoped that by examining women's past experiences, contemporary women could better understand why and how gender-based expectations had developed in their societies, as well as how they might reshape inherited—and typically restrictive—economic, social, and political roles in the future.

Today, some four decades after the feminist and social history movements gave new impetus to the study of women's history, there is a rich and continually growing body of work on all aspects of women's lives in the past. The Lucent Books Women in History series draws upon this abundant and diverse literature to introduce students to women's experiences within a variety of past cultures and time periods in terms of the distinct roles they filled. In their capacities as workers, activists, and artists, women excerted significant influence on important events whether they conformed to or broke from traditional roles. The Women in History titles depict extraordinary women who managed to attain positions of influence in their male-dominated societies, including such celebrated heroines as the feisty medieval queen Eleanor of Aquitaine, the brilliant propagandist of the American Revolution Mercy Otis Warren, and the courageous African American activist of the Civil War era, Harriet Tubman. Included as well are the stories of the ordinary—and often overlooked—women of the past who also helped shape their societies in myriad ways—moral, intellectual, and economic—without straying far from customary gender roles: the housewives and mothers, schoolteachers and church volunteers, midwives and nurses, and wartime camp followers.

In this series, readers will discover that many of these unsung women took more significant parts in the great political and social upheavals of their day than has often been recognized. In *Women of the American Revolution,* for example, students will learn how American housewives assumed a crucial role in helping the Patriots win the war against Britain. They accomplished this by planting and harvesting fields, producing and trading goods, and doing whatever else was necessary to maintain the family farm or business in the absence of their soldier husbands despite the heavy burden of housekeeping and child care duties they already bore. By their self-sacrificing actions, competence, and ingenuity, these anonymous heroines not only kept their families alive, but kept the economy of their struggling young nation going as well during eight long years of war.

Each volume in this series contains generous commentary from the works of respected contemporary scholars, but the Women in History series particularly emphasizes quotations from primary sources such as diaries, letters, and journals whenever possible to allow the women of the past to speak for themselves. These first-hand accounts not only help students to better understand the dimensions of women's daily spheres—the work they did, the organizations they belonged to, the physical hardships they faced—but also how they viewed themselves and their actions in the light of their society's expectations for their sex.

The distinguished American historian Mary Beard once wrote that women have always been a "force in history." It is hoped that the books in this series will help students to better appreciate the vital yet often little known ways in which women of the past have shaped their societies and cultures.

Introduction:
The War and the Women

❧

There was no such thing as a typical American woman of the mid–nineteenth century. The lives of the women of the time varied enormously. Differences in class, race, marital status, and education strongly affected the experience a woman would have; even the region of the country where a woman lived helped define who she was, how she thought, and what she did. The life of a Southern lady on a large plantation, for example, was not very similar to the life of a Northern immigrant woman. An educated young woman of Philadelphia or Boston did not have the same outlook or expectations as a middle-aged farm woman in the Midwest, and slave women had very little in common with the wives of wealthy industrialists.

To be sure, in a few broad ways the lives of women across the country were similar. Virtually all women, for instance, were expected to busy themselves with domestic tasks and ideals. Their focus was supposed to be on the home, and their interests were narrowly limited to matters of church and family. They were perceived as helpmates and nurturers, responsible for and well suited to domestic duties and childrearing. The wider world of politics, commerce, and industry, and the medical and legal professions was largely off limits to the women of the time.

Whether by choice or by tradition, most American women in pre–Civil War days followed that basic description of roles and responsibilities. This was true of women across economic, racial, and regional lines. Of course, many women were forced by economic necessity to work in fields and factories, and certain public activities, notably the writing of fiction and poetry, were not only acceptable but encouraged. Still, these were exceptions. For the most part, women were schooled to excel in the domestic realm, and they were expected to leave everything else in the hands of men.

The Civil War
Then, in 1861, the Civil War broke out, a devastating conflict that has been called

the single most important event in American history. The four years of fighting left one out of every five soldiers dead and hundreds of thousands wounded; thousands more civilians were left homeless and destitute. Indeed, the Civil War affected every American in some important way, directly or indirectly. That was true for both rich and poor; for both Southerners and Northerners; for both blacks and whites. And it was true for both men and women, as well.

Women, in fact, had extremely varied experiences of the Civil War. Some were involved in the war primarily as wives and mothers of men who fought. Others, in contrast, made their way to the front lines and served as scouts, spies, or even soldiers. Women acted as regimental cooks, ran farms and small businesses on the home front, and gathered supplies for the troops. Many slave women spent most of the war laboring on Southern plantations and planning a break for freedom. A few well-educated and well-informed women wrote articles and poems expressing political points of view. No two women shared precisely the same wartime experience.

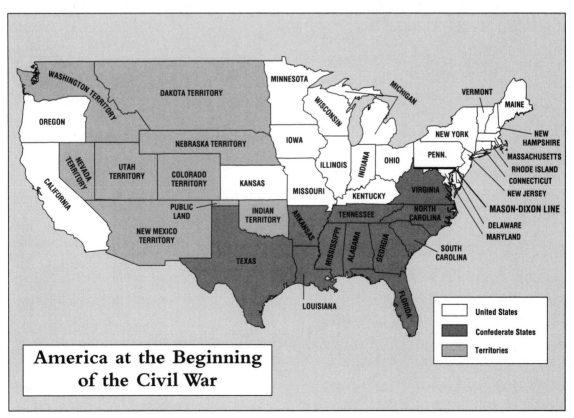

America at the Beginning of the Civil War

In 1861 women were expected to busy themselves with husbands, children, and household duties. The Civil War brought new and varied experiences to all American women, rich or poor, free or slave, Northern or Southern.

In one way or another, however, most women of the Civil War found themselves taking on roles traditionally filled by men. Whether giving political speeches, managing slaves, or serving as full-time nurses, women found themselves moving into a more public sphere and pushing the limits of traditional women's roles. Some found the changes wrenching and all but impossible. Others, though, found their new respon- sibilities liberating and tremendously exciting.

The women of the Civil War approached the conflict from multiple situations and perspectives. It is not sur- prising, then, that they took part in the war in many different ways. The war deeply influenced the lives of women all across the United States; in turn, the activities of women had an enormous impact on the waging of the war.

Chapter 1:
Women on the Northern Home Front

In some ways, the Civil War had less impact on the typical white woman of the North than it did on any other group of Americans. Where men of both the North and South were called upon to fight, women were barred from enlisting; as a result, women avoided the battlefield deaths, the squalid conditions of the army camps, and the gruesome and often permanent injuries suffered by men. In a war fought largely on Southern soil, many women of the South found their lives turned upside down by nearby battles and by advancing Union soldiers; Northern women, in contrast, mainly escaped the experience of being under fire. And because the war was fought, at least in part, over the issue of slavery, Northern African Americans found themselves much closer to the ideological center of the conflict than any Northern woman of the white majority.

But even if the white women of the North were not as directly affected by the war as most others, it would be a mistake to say that they were uninvolved. On the contrary, the experiences of Northern women at home were strongly connected with the events of the war. When the men of the community left to fight, the women who remained often took on new roles and discovered new ways of coping with everyday challenges of life. When men were wounded and died, wives and mothers had to deal with their fears and sorrows. Indeed, in a time of poor transportation and communication systems, following the war from a distance was at times harder than experiencing it firsthand.

Still, the women of the North were scarcely passive observers of the war. Even without leaving their home counties, large numbers of Northern women actively worked to help the war effort. Wealthy ladies and poor immigrant housewives alike took it upon themselves to sew, gather supplies, and solicit funds to support the Union troops. Others, championing the federal cause, gave lectures, penned patriotic ballads, and wrote letters to government officials urging action or voicing opinion. And many Northern women sacrificed family life, sometimes permanently, by encouraging their husbands and sons to join the conflict.

Patriotic Fervor

For most Northern women, the coming of the Civil War was accompanied by feelings of patriotic pride and excitement. Mary Livermore of Boston was one of innumerable Northern women who attended rallies designed to whip up pro-Union sentiment. Like most of the others, Livermore was moved by the experience. "I saw the dear banner of my country," she wrote about an April 1861 gathering, "rising higher and higher to the top of the flagstaff, fling out fold after fold to the damp air, and float proudly." Livermore was surprised by her reaction, since she had not been patriotic in the past. "Never before," she added, "had the national flag signified anything to me."[1]

In a blaze of nationalist feeling fueled by such rallies, women across the North eagerly urged their husbands and brothers to enlist in the Union army. Some men needed no encouragement, but many women cast rather forceful doubt on the motives and characters of those who did. "I wouldn't [even] look at a nonresistant,"[2] declared twenty-one-year-old Ellen Wright, referring to men who refused to enlist; and other Northern women echoed her sentiments. A small faction opposed the war on religious or personal grounds from the beginning. And as months of fighting became years and the realities of war became apparent, Northern women as well as men became less enthusiastic in their support. Still, the early days of the war saw considerable enthusiasm for the fight among the women of the Union.

In part, that enthusiasm was due to a misjudgment about the probable length of the war. During the first few weeks of the fighting, many Northern politicians and ordinary citizens believed that Union determination and firepower would swiftly overcome the South. If the war was to be short, then the danger was relatively low, and women could urge their husbands, sons, and sweethearts to join with faith in their well-being. As historian Agatha Young puts it with only minimal exaggeration, "Preparing a son for a war which would last three months, or a very little longer, was . . . not so different from preparing a boy to take part in the school play."[3]

The intense enthusiasm for the war prompted festive demonstrations of women's support for the troops. Some

Fresh recruits in the Union army are entertained by the women of Baltimore.

organized parties and parades for the soldiers as their units departed from home. One New York woman spent an entire morning preparing and wrapping beef sandwiches for the soldiers who passed through town on their way to the front. Especially in the earliest weeks of the war, women in small towns and major cities across the North participated in activities of this sort.

Soon many Northern women, however, turned to projects of greater practicality. Cheering at parades and handing out beef sandwiches were helpful and appropriate activities, but when the parades were over and the sandwiches had been eaten there was no obvious way to continue to support the troops. Some women, recognizing this lack of organization, formed local groups to address the problem. Instead of relying on haphazard efforts to encourage and comfort the soldiers, these women planned to set up networks among Northerners which would systematically funnel supplies to the men at the front on a continuing basis.

Barbara Frietschie

The North had several well-known heroines during the war—women whose loyalty and courage on the Union's behalf was celebrated in songs, poetry, and prose. In some cases, though, it has become difficult to distinguish fact from fiction. Among the most famous of these heroines—if heroine she actually was—was Barbara Frietschie, immortalized in a verse by New England poet John Greenleaf Whittier.

Born in Pennsylvania in 1766, Frietschie was living in the border town of Frederick, Maryland, a community with strongly divided sympathies, when the war broke out. In September 1862, a group of Southern soldiers marched through Frederick on its way to the Battle of Antietam. According to the story, Frietschie—a loyal Unionist—hung an American flag out of her window to show support for the North. When the Confederate commander, Stonewall Jackson, saw the flag, he ordered his troops to halt and fire. The resulting blast riddled the flag with bullets.

Frietschie then stuck her head out of the window and addressed Jackson's men. "Shoot, if you must, this old gray head," the poet Whittier had her saying, quoted in editor Edward T. James's *Notable American Women,* "But spare your country's flag." According to legend, the commander was moved by her courage and ordered his men to pass on by. "Who touches a hair of yon gray head," Whittier imagined Jackson telling his troops, "Dies like a dog! March on!"

The story was dramatic and inspiring. It was told frequently by Union sympathizers in Frederick and was spread throughout the North by Whittier's 1863 poem. Whether the event actually took place as described, though, is doubtful. Several sources suggest that the ninety-five-year-old Frietschie, who would die only three months after the Confederates marched through Frederick, was far too old and frail to have left her bed when the troops came through. Others point out that Jackson's route that day did not take him past Frietschie's house.

It is possible that the incident never occurred. It is also possible that it did take place, but that a woman other than Frietschie was actually involved. Some historians believe that the flag may have been displayed by a somewhat younger woman named Mary Quantrell instead. But for thousands of loyal Unionists, the truth of the story mattered less than its message: that Northern women were capable of great acts of courage in demonstrating their loyalty.

Soldiers' Aid Societies

The earliest of these organizations arose almost as soon as the war had begun. On April 15, 1861, just three days after the war's first shots had been fired, several women of Bridgeport, Connecticut, banded together to form a so-called soldiers' aid society. Within two weeks, similar societies—sometimes called bonnet brigades—were up and running in nearly every good-sized town in the North. "The Ladies of the city are requested to meet on Saturday afternoon at 3 o'clock in the Medical College Hall," read a typical notice appearing in the daily newspaper of Keokuk, Iowa, "for the purpose of forming a Volunteer Aid Society."[4]

The goal of the soldiers' aid societies was simple enough: to provide necessary goods and equipment for the soldiers. Because it was unclear how much support the government itself could or would provide, the women of the societies took on the responsibility of sending the men everything they might possibly need, from complete military uniforms to food packages. Most of these items had to be produced at home, and many were made by hand, piece by piece. The investment of time and energy was considerable: It could take fourteen hours just to sew one soldier's shirt.

Despite the amount of time the projects required, many Northern women threw themselves into the work. They tirelessly canvased friends and neighbors, asking them to help out by donating preserves or cutting bandages from scrap cloth. Once the women had enough supplies to fill a good-sized box, they would send it to the troops at the front, often with encouraging and patriotic notes attached. "Assure our brave men that gratitude to them mingles with our desire to serve our country,"[5] read the label on a box containing a hundred pairs of socks knitted by some Cincinnati women.

During the early days of the war, relief, soldiers' aid, and ladies societies were formed everywhere, meeting in parlors, churches, schools, and town halls. In Concord, Massachusetts, 140 women considered themselves regular members of the local organization, and another 60 attended meetings from time to time; that was out of a total town population of less than 2,500. As one Union man admiringly wrote, "Men did not take to the musket more commonly than women took to the needle."[6] From Maine to Minnesota, box after box was quickly filled with all manner of supplies and shipped to the needy men at the front.

Problems and Successes

Most of the goods soldiers received were very much appreciated. The soldiers had little in the way of luxuries

Northern women sew soldiers' uniforms and exhort their men to enlist in the army.

and not nearly enough necessities, so they welcomed the gift of a pair of shoes or a box of candy. Unfortunately, not all shipments were appropriate. Some Northern women sent along chickens, which spoiled on the way to the front, or butter, which had a tendency to melt. And some of the clothing was so poorly made as to be completely useless. One soldier received a pair of pants that had apparently been constructed backwards. As one observer wrote, he needed to "stand on his head to button them."[7]

The soldiers' aid societies had been formed to encourage donations and to make sure that supplies were delivered efficiently. Before long, however, signifi-

cant problems became apparent. Although the volunteer organizations were well meaning and often quite well structured, their efforts were not coordinated. As a result, some regiments got more supplies than they needed, while others went without. Likewise, when one organization learned what sorts of items were most useful or how best to ship them, there was no easy way to share this new knowledge with other societies.

By the summer of 1861, therefore, several national organizations had been formed to take over the task of soliciting and distributing the necessary supplies. Many of these groups were run and founded primarily by women. "We began life in a little room which contained two tables, one desk, half a dozen chairs, and a map on the wall," recalled Louisa Lee Schuyler, who was active in the Women's Central Association of Relief. "We sent out circulars, wrote letters, looked out of the windows at the passing regiments, and talked about our work, sometimes hopefully, sometimes despairingly."[8] Their work did pay off, though; before long Schuyler's group was one of several that provided useful organization and valuable help to the troops of the Union.

Few soldiers' aid societies were still in business at the end of the war. By 1862, most of these independent groups had been supplanted by the U.S. Sanitary Commission, a civilian organization approved by the War Department's Medical Bureau. The Sanitary Commission inspected army camps and hospitals, collected and distributed a huge variety of supplies, and offered services to needy soldiers. While the Sanitary Commission was governed by a board consisting entirely of men, it depended on female workers, members, and contributors, and the influence of women in the founding and running of the group was clear. With the rise of the Sanitary Commission, the membership and importance of the volunteer groups run exclusively by women

The U.S. Sanitary Commission, although governed by a male board, was dependent on the work and contributions of women.

diminished, although several of these organizations continued to function as a part of the commission, and a few operated independently until the war was at an end.

The original soldiers' aid societies, run and established by women, and the Sanitary Commission all proved extremely important to the North. They gave tangible support to the soldiers while providing an acceptable outlet for the energies of Northern women. Many of the women who participated in the bonnet brigades had never been so directly involved in national life before, and they took pleasure in the role they were able to play. As one woman who visited a Union hospital proudly reported, "The last sound that reached my ears was cheers for the Sanitary Commission and the women at home."[9]

Women in the Public Eye

The women who organized and ran the bonnet brigades were indeed stepping into public affairs in a way that women rarely had done in the past. A few Northern women, however, took on even more active political roles. Wholehearted supporters of the Northern cause, these women wrote, lectured, and busied themselves with political questions. Many of them became well-known figures in the civic life of the North.

Political activism came naturally to some women who had been staunch abolitionists before the war—those who had worked for the elimination of slavery. The women who supported abolition did not slacken their efforts once the war began. If anything, they increased their political activity. While some continued to limit their lobbying to the freeing of slaves, others now took on a broader perspective. They urged more general support for the Union troops and for the ruling Republican Party as well.

Anna Dickinson, for example, who had contributed an article to an antislavery publication when she was just fourteen years old, spent much of the war giving lectures throughout the North. She was a dramatic speaker with a particular flair for sarcasm and insult, a talent she used against Southerners as well as Northerners who did not support the war effort. In 1864, only twenty-five years old, Dickinson was invited to speak in the U.S. Capitol building, where her audience included congressmen and President Lincoln himself.

Other women had different ways of showing their commitment to the Northern cause. Julia Ward Howe, a well-off resident of New York City, wrote the words to the pro-Union "Battle Hymn of the Republic," one of the most popular anthems of the Civil

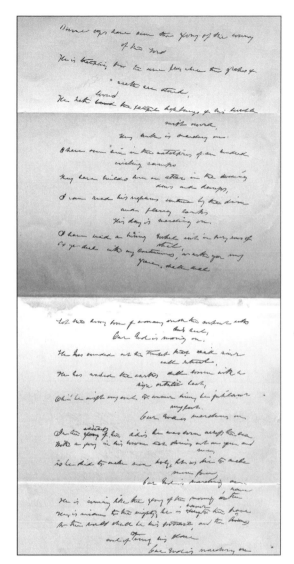

Northern women also made literary contributions to the war effort. Pictured at left is the first draft of Julia Ward Howe's "Battle Hymn of the Republic," one of the most popular Civil War anthems. Anna Dickinson (above) was only fourteen years old when she wrote her first antislavery article.

War—or any other war. Mary Abigail Dodge, another writer, published articles urging Northern women to support the Union at all costs. "O women," she wrote meaningfully, "the hour has need of you."[10]

Among the most interesting of all Northern women during the war was Anna Ella Carroll of Maryland. A veteran writer and lecturer on political issues, Carroll produced two political pamphlets in 1861, each discussing the constitutional questions surrounding secession and the federal government's right to put down the rebellion. The following year, she concerned herself with questions of military strategy. After the war, in fact, Carroll claimed to have thought up a Union plan to invade the South along the Tennessee River, a campaign that was successfully carried out in 1862. Carroll's assertion has been hotly debated, and direct evidence for her role in the plan is scanty. Nevertheless, Carroll's interest in military planning was unusual for the time, and the pamphlets she wrote were undeniably important.

Hardships at Home

Public figures such as Carroll, Dickinson, and Schuyler were highly influential, but they made up only a small proportion of Northern women. For most women of the North, such activities would have been too far outside accepted standards of womanly behavior. Moreover, many women who would have relished the opportunity to write, speak, or strategize did not have the time or the energy. Much as they might have wanted to write anti-Southern poetry or organize thousands of women into soldiers' aid societies, they had more pressing responsibilities.

The initial call for troops caused thousands of Northern men to enlist. In some towns and villages, more than half the able-bodied men went to war. The absence of the men changed life considerably for the women who remained. Those whose husbands had worked outside the home faced a major loss of income; army wages were typically lower than the pay the men were giving up. Women whose husbands were merchants or farmers did not necessarily suffer as large a drop in income, but they had to take over their husbands' share of the work in order to survive.

Indeed, added work was a reality for many women of the North. Women whose husbands had managed the money, disciplined the children, and made most of the important family decisions now found that they needed to take over these tasks. These duties, furthermore, did not replace the standard female responsibilities of washing, cooking, and cleaning. The result was that many Northern women had to work as they had never worked before in their lives.

Worse still, the war disrupted the flow of goods and supplies throughout the North. The economic effects of this disruption were alarming. Prices rose across the Northern states, in some cases more than doubling, and shortages were common. Most of these shortages involved luxuries rather than necessities, and most likewise made items difficult, though not impossible, to find. Still, at best the shortages were inconvenient. Well-off Washington women made do with dresses till they nearly wore out, and some New York families could get only half the butter they were accustomed to. And at worst the shortages threatened the health and nutrition of Northerners. Food costs before the war had prevented some families from buying all they needed. Rising prices, especially in cities far from farms, forced some Northern women to cut back even more.

Struggling to Survive

For those Northern women who were unaccustomed to being in charge and overwhelmed by the duties of managing alone, economic hardship and extra responsibilities amounted to a struggle for survival. Some rural women abandoned their family farms and headed for the cities, hoping to find paying work. While many of these women did find jobs as clerks, factory hands, and domestic servants, their earning power was slight, and they suffered the added burden of being friendless in an unfamiliar place.

Women already living in poverty were most severely affected by the economic hardship and by the absence of their husbands, but middle-class women often suffered as well. Because the government at the time did not offer social services such as welfare benefits or food stamps, needy women had few options. Many were forced to rely on the kindness or charity of friends and families. Unfortunately, new arrangements were often less than satisfactory. When families moved in together, living quarters were cramped and supplies stretched thin, privacy was nonexistent, and tensions frequently strained relationships.

The North also had a number of privately run charities. Most of these were already well established, but some sprang up during the war. Sponsored by religious or civic groups and often organized by women, these charities gave food

Many rural women struggled to survive economically during the war and were forced into the cities in search of jobs like this one in a shoe factory.

and clothing to those in need of help. Some also could assist women who wanted to find work. A few communities took this work quite seriously, too, even choosing to help the local needy before they supported the Union troops. "We have just been making contributions to releave our Soldiers families," wrote a woman from Newport, New York, in answer to a request for supplies from a national soldiers' aid society. "They were *suffering,* but we will do for you as soon as we can."[11]

However, the budgets of these charities were severely limited. As a result, those who sought help got little more than the bare minimum necessary to sustain life. Moreover, asking for help could be quite difficult for women who were brought up to be self-reliant. Out of pride, some refused to make any requests at all until the need was absolutely dire. Even those who did seek help often did so on the condition that they remain anonymous. To many women, privacy was essential, and only charity workers knew of their need for assistance.

"Take Your Gun and Go"

Although some women had a terribly difficult time once the men had gone away, other women thrived on the increased responsibility. They were determined to be successful even with their men gone to war. "Take your gun and go, John," urged the female narrator in a song popular in the North. "For Ruth can drive the oxen, John, and I can use the hoe."[12] Plenty of actual Northern women shared this fictional woman's confidence, and many of them did extremely well for themselves. That was particularly true of farm women. On a visit to the Midwest, New Englander Mary Livermore reported her surprise at having seen a "great number" of women "engaged in . . . planting, cultivating and harvesting."[13] Faced with a choice between hard work and giving up, these women chose the work.

Other women likewise found themselves able to grow and flourish despite—or perhaps because of—the harsh demands of life during the Civil War. Northern women ran businesses, took jobs outside the home, handled money matters for the first time, and discovered that they enjoyed the responsibilities and the freedom to try new things. Some were helped by instructions from their absent husbands. "Tell John Wilber to get notes of all those that do not pay those bills promptly," directed Lydia Edgerton's husband from his regiment's encampment. "Have Wright get Charlie a pair of Boots as soon as you can spare the money."[14] But even in these cases, the ultimate responsibility for managing matters lay with the women.

Even the wealthiest, most pampered women were forced to become more resourceful during the war. In 1863, one lady of Philadelphia was distressed when a sudden shortage made laundry soap unavailable. But she was not helpless; accustomed to shortages after two years of fighting, she cheerfully learned to make her own—and vowed that never again would she waste it as she had done before.

"Weeping, Sad and Lonely"

Still, no matter how well the women handled the details of everyday life, the war created terrible tension and anxiety. Most women in the North had close relatives at the front. They keenly felt the absence of their loved ones; thoughts and concerns for them dominated the women's emotional lives. There was no doubt that it took courage to adjust to the separation, and some observers thought *courage* was not nearly a strong enough word. "For women to send forth their husbands, sons, brothers, and lovers to the fearful chances of the battle-field," wrote Mary Livermore, "involves another kind of heroism."[15]

Separations were of uncertain length. Men might come home for an occasional leave of absence, but other

Many Civil War songs, poems, and works of art, such as the one pictured here, expressed women's longing and fear for their absent men.

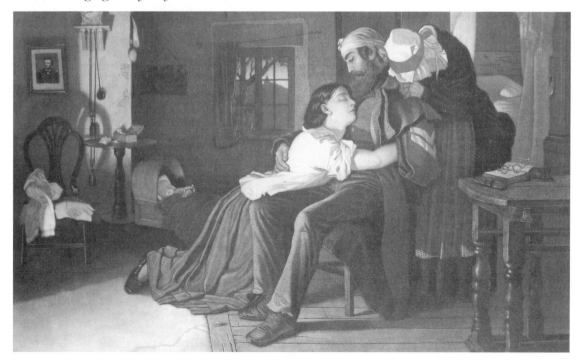

than that, communication between home and soldier was possible only by letter. Mail service was both spotty and slow, and illiterate women who could not find someone to take dictation did not communicate with their husbands at all. Still, many women found it a true comfort to have even such limited contact as this. "Received a letter from James," wrote Mary Warden Bingham of Michigan in her diary after a note arrived from her soldier son. "How dear these letters are."[16]

The Civil War was a war of romantic imagery, of heroic soldiers and adventurous ideals, and the women who remained at home often indulged in sentimental thoughts and fancies. Many poems and songs of the day dealt with the parting of lovers and the resulting feelings of grief and loyalty. In one exceptionally popular song, a woman sang to her absent beloved:

Weeping, sad and lonely,

Hopes and fears how vain!

When this cruel war is over,

Praying that we meet again![17]

For many Northern women, lyrics such as these expressed their feelings about the war and made the sorrow a bit easier to face.

Wounds and Deaths

A common worry among the women of the North was that their loved ones would be wounded in battle. They had reason to be concerned. Many soldiers returned home missing an arm or a leg or with wounds that permanently compromised their health. Some Northern women hurried to the front when they got the news of a serious injury. Unfortunately, for most women a trip of this length was too costly and too time consuming; they had to trust that their men would somehow manage to get well.

But as the song "Weeping, Sad and Lonely" suggests, a woman's greater war-related fear was learning that a loved one was dead. Comforting as letters could be, many wives and mothers received them with a certain amount of dread. Sometimes, they knew, the mail carried news of a loved one's death. For some women the news arrived with a distressing regularity: Nancy Rhodes of Maine was one of several Northern women said to have lost four sons to the war.

The sorrow over the deaths was compounded by several factors. For one, many women had moved away from family and friends for economic reasons, so they were forced to grieve more or less alone. "If I could only have had some friend here to talk to about him," mourned a displaced Union woman after the death

Because fallen soldiers often were buried near the battlefields and hospitals where they died rather than being returned home, many families mourned loved ones from great distances.

of a relative, "I think I could have borne it better."[18] For another, the men usually died a great distance from home. That made it impracticable to return the corpses for burial at home, and women often lacked a sense of closure when the men were laid to rest near the battlefield or hospital where they died.

Finally, Civil War deaths were particularly hard on Northern women because the system of notification was poor. Official letters informing next of kin of the death of a husband or son were supposed to be timely but often were not. Sometimes it was difficult to identify a corpse, especially after major battles involving many casualties. Slow and haphazard mail deliveries worsened the situation. The result was that some women endured agonizing months of waiting before official word arrived that their loved one was dead.

Some Northern women were able to rationalize the losses of their relatives. "Two sons I have already given," one Philadelphia woman was quoted as saying, "and four grandsons; nor do I regret the gift . . . for the country must and shall be preserved."[19] But as the war dragged on, most women were unable to view the deaths so philosophically or see them as a necessary part of a greater good. It was hard to see death as a glorious sacrifice for a noble cause when faced with the very real loss of a beloved family member. Much more common was the reaction of Mary

Gettysburg

V ery few women north of the border states came under fire during the Civil War. But the casualty list at Gettysburg did include one Pennsylvania woman, Jennie Wade. When the battle came near, Wade could not leave her house; she was at home with her mother and a sister, and the sister had just given birth.

Wade busied herself baking bread for the Union soldiers, but when a shell struck the house she realized that the family was in danger. Quickly Wade settled her mother, sister, and the new baby in the cellar. She returned to the kitchen after a few minutes, however, intending to check on the dough. It was a mistake: As she stood over the oven, her fingers in the bread dough, another shot came into the kitchen and killed her. Wade was the only woman known to die in the Battle of Gettysburg.

Warden Bingham. "My life seems very monotonous," she wrote three months after receiving word of the death of her soldier son, "and I wonder sometimes why I am left when of so little use."[20]

Tragedy and Coping

Bingham's sense of loss was shared throughout the North, which lost 360,000 men to battle deaths and disease. The death of a loved one was perhaps the hardest of the difficulties Northern women faced, but it was by no means the only one. Many women suffered from economic hardship; many women had to swallow their pride and beg for food or shelter from relatives or strangers; many women missed their husbands more than they could put into words.

But at the same time, the war provided Union women with an unexpected opportunity for personal growth. Thousands of women across the North learned that they could indeed run a farm, manage the finances, or make effective and important decisions. The war also provided women with the chance to move, however tentatively, into the public sphere. The women who lectured, wrote, and lobbied for political causes were at the head of the column; but even the women who actively participated in soldiers' aid programs were moving beyond the traditional roles of women in previous decades.

Chapter 2:
Women on the Southern Home Front

In the middle of the Civil War, a Kentucky woman named Issa Breckinridge left her home and traveled north to Canada. Although Kentucky never seceded from the Union, it was a slaveholding state where loyalties were sharply divided; Breckinridge, like many of her border-state neighbors, was soldily in the camp of the Confederacy. She cheered Southern military victories, corresponded regularly with her husband, a Confederate army officer stationed deep in Confederate territory, and thought of herself as a Southerner.

Breckinridge's journey to Canada, however, took her through Union territory in the Midwest. There she was startled to see people going about their business as if nothing important were happening beyond the boundaries of their towns, in sharp contrast to the upheaval in her pro-Confederate region of Kentucky. It was astonishing, she wrote, "to find how little the people of the North feel this war." She was jealous, too, to see that "everything [looked] so prosperous—everybody so happy."[21]

Breckinridge was mistaken, of course; the people of the North felt the effects of the war quite strongly. Still, Breckinridge can be forgiven for her comments. In comparison with the people she knew best—the white women of the South—there is no doubt that the Northerners were much better off. The life of a Southern woman at home during the war was noticeably more precarious and more difficult than the life of her Northern counterpart. In some ways, in fact, Confederate women suffered even more than did the soldiers of the South. In the words of one historian, the women of the Confederacy had to bear "the harder part of the war."[22]

"God Will Protect the Right"

Certainly, some Southern women did not support the Confederacy, and some Southern women opposed the Civil War.

Both were more common in the hillier regions of the South, where ownership of slaves was relatively rare. Still, the women of the South on the whole were intensely supportive of the war, at least early on. If anything, they were even more zealous about the conflict than were the women of the North. Many Confederate women eagerly urged their husbands and brothers to go and fight. These women steadfastly refused to hear any doubts, complaints, or objections.

Southern women pushed their men to "do their duty" to defend their wives, mothers, and sisters.

Women of the Civil War

Southerners' fervor was intensified in part by their belief that the South, unlike the North, was fighting to preserve its identity and its way of life. Southerners believed that their region was being unfairly treated and that their rights as a people were threatened; in their eyes, they were defending their homeland against outside invaders. The women of the Confederacy were as rebellious as any Southern man. As they saw it, Southern ideals had to be defended at any cost. "Our cause is a just and holy one," one Mississippi woman wrote with assurance in 1862, "and God will protect the right."[23]

There was a cultural reason, too, for the widespread support of the war among Confederate women. Southerners frequently viewed Southern men as courageous defenders of Southern women. Men were supposed to fight in order to protect their wives, sisters, and mothers. It was up to women to push men to do their duty—and to accept the hardships stoically when they did. "I had no tears to shed," Catherine Edmondston reported proudly after her husband left for the front. "I would not have him here, would not have him fail in one duty, falter in one step."[24]

But if women publicly had no tears to shed, the private diaries and letters of Southern women often revealed a sharp sense of loss when a loved one went off to battle. A husband or a son could be away for months, even years. Indeed, there was no guarantee he would come back at all. "What do I care for patriotism?" one South Carolina woman asked plaintively. "My husband is my country. What is country to me if he be killed?"[25] Still, sentiments such as these were best kept private in the early months of the war.

Love and Loss

As the war progressed, however, the enthusiasm began to diminish. It became apparent to Confederate women that the burdens of the war were borne disproportionately by the South. That realization did not necessarily reduce the support many of the women had for the war; most Southerners on the home front held out hope for a Confederate victory until the fighting was nearly over. It did, however, make it easier for women to admit that they were suffering, and more likely that they would express themselves openly.

One reason for the war's greater impact in the South was the far higher proportion of the white male population called to active duty. Historians estimate that about one in ten Union men served in the army; in contrast, virtually every able-bodied Southern man sooner or later served in the Confederate army,

"The Rush of Yankee Ruffians"

Confederate women could only look on as the troops led by General William Tecumseh Sherman destroyed property on their sweep through Georgia and the Carolinas. An anonymous woman of Sandersville, Georgia, tells this account, quoted in Katharine M. Jones's *When Sherman Came:*

Now the rush of Yankee ruffians! Our doors were all barred and locked, but they shook them so we knew they would soon break them down. So mother and I went to open them. Fierce-looking men confronted me—the veranda was full. . . .

All day long, the men and wagons poured into the town. "Rip! Rip," went the yard and garden fences, as they tore them down and pitched their white-winged tents at our very doorsteps—no yards, no gardens, were spared in our ill-fated village. Now the soldiers, with hateful leers from their red eyes, would walk up to the steps of the back veranda, on which we stood, and throwing down the hams and shoulders of our meat, which they had found, would cut them up with savage delight, in our very faces. Next they found the sugar, flour, lard, salt, syrup, which mother had stored away in a cellar, dug beneath one of the Negro houses, by a trusty servant.

Even in the midst of warfare and wanton destruction, though, the writer noted an act of kindness. The Federals had left so little food that she had no way to feed her young son. Noticing this, a young Union soldier promised to share some of his own rations with her. Later that evening, he returned with flour and coffee—enough to keep the little boy alive for another day.

including, by the end of the war, old men and boys assigned to guard duty. While about one in seven Union soldiers died in the war, one in four Confederate soldiers died in battle or of wounds or disease, partly because military medical care was inferior in the South.

Thus, a much larger share of Confederate women experienced the loss or injury of a loved one than did the women of the North. To make matters worse, information about deaths and wounds was often inaccurate. One Southern woman, after being informed that her son was dead, suddenly received word that it was all a mistake. "She fell on her knees with a shout of joy," an observer reported. "The swing-back of the pendulum from the scene of weeping . . . was very exciting." But that was not the end of the story. "In the midst of this hubbub," the observer added grimly, "the hearse drove up with the poor boy in his metallic coffin."[26]

The death of a sweetheart, husband, or son was an ever-present possibility for Southern women. Some tried to accept the loss stoically, others sought comfort in brave and patriotic sentiments. "Hearts do break in silence, without a word or a sigh," mused Southern diarist Mary Chesnut. Like many women of the time, Chesnut kept a detailed diary. A woman of wealth and privilege, and an ardent Confederate and defender of slavery, Chesnut lost no close relatives in the fighting but recorded her sorrow and sympathy for those who did. "I think if I consider the long array of those bright youths and loyal men who have gone to their deaths almost before my very eyes," she wrote, "my heart might break, too."[27]

Slaves and Plantations

Being left at home proved difficult for Confederate women for other reasons, too. Southern society was overwhelmingly rural, and the plantations could be quite large. Women whose husbands had gone to battle sometimes had no near neighbors on whom they could rely. Nor did the Confederacy have large cities offering paying work, although a few needy women did find jobs in factories, schools, or the national government. Moreover, social service efforts in the South were weak. The distances between communities and the small size of settlements all worked against the development of systems to help those in need.

Life among the wealthier women of the South was complicated, too, by the presence of slaves. During the war, many women of the Confederacy were called upon to take over the running of farms and plantations. Most found it hard enough to manage farm machinery and bookkeeping, and having to feed, clothe, and discipline the slaves proved much more difficult. Few upper- or middle-class Confederate women had much experience handling slaves who worked in the fields. Nor did they know how to manage an entire plantation.

Some of these women, like their counterparts in the North, took on their new tasks with remarkable courage and enthusiasm. Eliza Prince, for example, grew so confident of her own abilities that she fired her overseer, a white man charged with handling the slaves, and managed without him. Leila Callaway's

Some upper- and middle-class Southern women found themselves in charge of their plantation's slaves and male overseers when their husbands went to war.

husband wrote her a letter in which he started to offer her advice about managing that fall's harvest. Then he stopped. "Dear me," he wrote instead, "why should I advise an experienced farmer like yourself?"[28]

But women who adhered strictly to traditional Southern values were less successful. Ladies of the South were not supposed to busy themselves with so-called masculine concerns such as running a business or disciplining slaves. Some women found it difficult to move beyond

these expected roles, especially where slavery was concerned. One Alabama woman spoke for many when she said that she could not possibly learn how to manage the slaves, and a Georgia woman rented her slaves out to another farmer for the duration of the war.

Slaves presented another problem, too: Some Southerners feared that the slaves might use the war as an opportunity to stage a revolt. The Confederate government, fearing that chaos would result if white males were removed from the region's biggest plantations, offered exemptions from military service to those men who owned twenty or more slaves. However, as the pressing need for troops grew, more and more owners, managers, and overseers were drawn away. The result, for some women, was fear bordering on panic. "We know not [at] what moment we may be hacked to death in the most cruel manner by our slaves,"[29] worried Keziah Brevard of South Carolina.

Many women of the slaveholding South did not share Brevard's concerns. Indeed, Confederate women frequently spoke with pride of the loyalty of their slaves. "We felt no fear of the slaves," wrote memoirist Parthenia Hague, twenty-three years old when the war began and living on her family plantation in southern Alabama. "The idea of any harm happening through them never entered our minds."[30] Still, many slaveholding women of the South tempered their statements. To some, the slaves' demeanor seemed almost eerily calm as the war raged all around them. "Are they stolidly stupid," wondered Mary Chesnut, "or wiser than we are, silent and strong, biding their time?"[31]

Shortages

Dealing with the slaves, managing farms, and coping with the possibility of a loved one's death all seemed difficult enough for Southern women. As the war continued, though, these worries were often supplanted by issues of immediate survival. Foremost among these were shortages of food, clothing, and other important materials. These scarcities began to arise very early in the war. By the middle of the conflict, they had caused major changes in the lifestyles of the women of the South.

The reasons for the shortages were simple enough. The eleven seceding states were overwhelmingly agricultural. The North contained most of the nation's factories, mines, and transportation systems. When shipments from the North stopped, Southerners had trouble getting raw materials and finished goods to supply their armies and their civilian populations. Moreover, Union ships blockaded Confederate ports early in the war, preventing Southerners from importing goods from Europe or from sympathetic Northern merchants. From time to time, a rebel ship could run the blockade and bring new materials into the Confederacy, but the volume of goods obtained in this way was small and uncertain.

Shortages thus permeated every aspect of Southern daily life. Such useful and common materials as paper, kerosene, and buttons were hard to find or simply unavailable. Prices rose sharply throughout the South: At various times a toothbrush might sell for $2.50, a dress for $190, and coffee for $70 a pound. Costs as high as those put many goods out of reach for all but the wealthiest citizens—if the goods could be obtained at all. "I never realized the varied needs of civilization," mourned one woman in Arkansas. "Every day something is out."[32]

Clothing shortages presented an especially acute problem for Southern women. Ready-made dresses, shoes, and even underwear could not be purchased during much of the war, except at exorbitant prices. The only alternative, for most women, was to sew their own. This was a definite hardship, especially for those women who had become used to store-bought goods. The situation was even more difficult because the South had a shortage of cloth and sewing materials as well. Most of the available fabric was rough and uncomfortable, and women were understandably reluctant to wear it. And needles and pins were hard to find; by the end of the war a set of pins could cost $5.

Some Confederate women nevertheless were able to carry through their

Making Do

Confederate women found ingenious ways of replacing common household objects made unavailable by the blockades. In this excerpt from Parthenia Hague's *A Blockaded Family*, Hague describes one way in which the residents of her southern Alabama town coped with the lack of buttons:

Thread that we spun at home was used for making buttons. The process was simple. A small reed, or, if that was wanting, a large-sized broom-straw, could be used; around this the thread for such buttons would be wound till of sufficient bulk; it was then slid from the reed; the button-hole stitch was used here again, and was thickly worked around the eyelet made by the reed; the eyelet was crossed with thread stronger than that of which the button was formed, for the purpose of attaching it to the garment. . . . After we had thickly worked the button-hole stitch around the eyelet, [we] took thread colored to blend with the warp and woof and again lightly overcast the button, so that the drab showed only as the background.

Buttons in the South, Hague reported, were also made from pine bark, pasteboard, gourd shells, varnished wood, and persimmon seeds.

projects with creativity and good humor. When cloth was difficult to get, the women of the South used curtains, tablecloths, and bedsheets to construct skirts and underwear. Many Confederates rediscovered the arts of weaving and spinning. Inventive women combined two old pairs of shoes, matching the less-damaged sole of one with the relatively intact upper part of the other. "Each woman and girl her own shoemaker," Parthenia Hague recalled with pride. "Away with bought shoes; we want none of them!"[33]

But resorting to handmade, or homespun, clothes could be both wearying and frustrating. Many women, unused to sewing, spent long hours creating even the simplest of outfits, and the finished results were neither comfortable nor flattering. Some women were able to see their labors as an example of their patriotism. Still, many others found themselves wishing for the old days. "I can stand patched-up dresses," admitted Eliza Andrews of Georgia in her journal, "but I can't help feeling vulgar and common in coarse underclothes."[34]

Food

The shortage of clothing, though, was merely an annoyance compared with the much more serious shortage of food. Like cloth, many staples of the Southern diet were imported from the North. But because of the blockades, they were only available in small and expensive quantities. And while Southern farms continued to produce corn, pork, and sugar, too much Confederate acreage was given over to inedible crops such as cotton and tobacco. The food produced was not nearly enough to feed a hungry nation.

As food shortages grew common, the women of the Confederacy longed for the more varied meals they had eaten in days past. One family, unable to buy meat, lived almost exclusively on okra soup and tomatoes. Others ate cornbread at every meal, supplemented by peas and an occasional piece of fatty bacon. Butter and molasses were luxuries. Coffee was so scarce that some families made their own substitute from okra seeds or dried yams. "Browned wheat, meal, and burnt corn made passable beverages," recalled Parthenia Hague. "Even meal-bran was browned and used for coffee if other substitutes were not available."[35]

The shortage of food had an impact even on the wealthiest of Confederates. When there was little food to be had, no amount of money could persuade shopkeepers and ordinary citizens to part with their share. Hague reported that obtaining a barrel of flour was cause for celebration among the wealthy in her part of Alabama. And those who could still afford luxuries could not afford very many of them. Constance Cary, a well-off Virginia woman, wrote that she never finished a meal in early 1865 "without wishing there were more of it."[36]

But the hardships faced by poor and middle-class women were much worse. The lack of nutrition threatened many Southern women with outright starvation. Formerly proud and self-sufficient women did whatever they had to in order to avoid that fate. Elizabeth Meriwether not only traded her clothing and household objects for food, but she stole corn from a nearby farmer as well. Harriet Lang threw away a piece of stale bread; deciding later that she could not afford to let it go to waste, she fished it out of the trash, brushed off the ants, and ate it.

"It Is Not Naughtiness"

Constant hunger had many unpleasant effects on adult women, but its impact was worse on their children. Mothers were powerless to intervene as their sons and daughters grew thin and begged for food. The children's suffering drove many women to despair. One woman started to spank her misbehaving daughter, but changed her mind when she realized how little the girl had been given to eat. "I cannot [punish] my poor little half-starved children," she said. "It is not naughtiness, it is hunger."[37]

In most cases, the women of the South did manage to keep themselves and their children alive. But the psychological and physical costs were enormous. As the war continued and morale sank, more and more women insisted their husbands come home to take care of their families. "We have nothing in the house to eat but a little bit of meal," a Virginia woman wrote her soldier husband. If he failed to return home immediately, she added, it would be too late: She and her children would be "in the old grave yard with your ma and pa."[38]

By the middle of the war, a few desperate Southern women resorted to criminal acts. In Savannah, Mobile, and other cities across the South, angry women raided shops and government storehouses in search of food. These so-called bread riots represented vandalism and theft, to be sure; but to the starving citizens who took part, the crimes were justified. There was no other way they could feed their families. A loaf of bread, said one Richmond woman about an 1863 riot, "is little enough for the government to give us after it has taken all our men."[39]

The same scene occurred in rural areas, too, as food became more and more scarce. In many parts of the South, hungry women roamed together through the countryside as harvest time neared. They

By the middle of the war the same Southern women who had pushed their men to join the Confederate army were raiding shops and government warehouses to feed themselves and their starving children.

Arrival of the Yankees

The greatest danger faced by Confederate women, though, involved their proximity to the fighting. The North, with a decided edge in military power, was on the offensive to recapture the rebel states. As a result, the largest share of the fighting, by far, took place in the South. Nearly all Southern states saw major battles and lengthy campaigns, and large chunks of the original Confederate territory spent much of the war in Union hands. The advance of Northern soldiers therefore affected thousands of Southern women.

In some parts of the South, Northern invaders moved in without much resistance from overburdened Confederate troops. While the shifting of power in such cases was relatively peaceful, women in these occupied areas chafed under the rule of Northerners. Angered by the ease with which Union troops had taken over New Orleans, for instance, the women of that city took out their frustrations on Northern soldiers in dozens of small but humiliating ways. Women regularly got off streetcars if a Yankee soldier got on, and several ladies

swarmed onto the plantations belonging to wealthy farmers and carried home what produce they could. Confederate officials tried to stop the mobs, both in urban and in rural areas. But the damage indicated the extent of the hunger—and the degree to which the women of the South were becoming unwilling to put patriotic sentiment ahead of their personal needs.

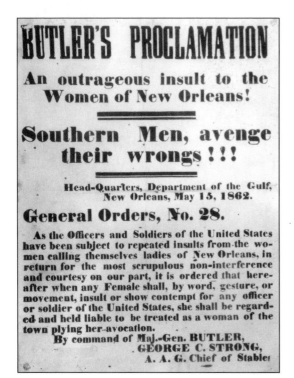

A Southern flyer calls for revenge on occupying Union general Butler for his remarks about the women of New Orleans.

of the town were known for emptying their chamber pots on passing Unionists' heads.

Indeed, women across the South frequently engaged in verbal and occasional physical attacks on Northern soldiers stationed in their communities, but women usually enjoyed a certain immunity from reprisals. "I have three sons fighting against you," one Louisiana woman screamed at a Union officer, "and you have robbed me, beggared me!"[40] Despite her outburst, the officer remained scrupulously polite. In 1861, future confederate spy Belle Boyd of Martinsburg, which is now in West Virginia, shot and killed a Northern soldier who was insulting her mother—and suffered no consequences whatever.

To be sure, not all Southern white women resented the occupiers. There were two main reasons why some did not. The first was self-preservation. For the poorest women in particular, the coming of the Yankees signified food. It was common knowledge that the Union armies were well provisioned. If shortages were bad enough, Confederate women were not above requesting help. Very often, they received it, too. Indeed, while many Southern women fled at the approach of the federal army, some actually moved north to meet the oncoming soldiers.

The second reason was romance. Despite the war, Americans on both sides shared a common language, heritage, and history. Contact between Union troops garrisoned in the South and the Southern civilian population was inevitable. Young, unattached men and women in occupied communities sometimes put politics aside, fell in love, and married. One Nashville woman sorrowfully reported that a friend, once a staunch Confederate, had "gone the way of all flesh and married an officer with that detestable eagle on his shoulder."[41]

Refugees

But few Southern women experienced the arrival of Union troops benignly. Some women found themselves caught literally in the crossfire between the two armies. Others discovered that their homes and property lay directly in the path of Union columns. The sudden arrival of the Northern army typically filled Southern women with fear and alarm. The question of protection was uppermost in these women's minds. "No one was left to meet the Federal army, should it pass by on our road," wrote

---

The Siege of Vicksburg

In late May 1863, the Union army laid siege to the Confederate city of Vicksburg, Mississippi. First, Northern soldiers blocked all exits leading from the community. Then they began a steady barrage of shots at the city, which was located on bluffs above the Mississippi River. During the next six weeks the inhabitants of Vicksburg—many of them women—suffered hardships unimagined by most other Americans during the war. Their food ran so low that many residents ate mule meat or caught and cooked rats. The constant gunfire created terrible psychological distress. Even their homes were unsafe: Most soon moved into their cellars or into caves dug out in the sides of the bluffs, where they presented a less-obvious target.

For the sake of their families, many Vicksburg women tried their best to be brave. Some succeeded, but as one resident realized, quoted in Agatha Young's *The*

Women and the Crisis, it was almost impossible to remain cool and collected for long.

A horrible day. The most horrible yet for me, because I've lost my nerve. We were all in the cellar, when a shell came tearing through the roof, burst upstairs, tore up that room, and the pieces [came] through both floors down into the cellar. . . . This was tangible proof the cellar was no place of protection from them. On the heels of this came Mr. J to tell us that young Mrs. P had had her thigh-bone crushed. When Martha went for the milk she came back horror-stricken to tell us the black girl there had her arm taken off by a shell. For the first time I quailed . . . [I] seemed to realize that something worse than death might come: I might be crippled and not killed. Life, without all one's powers and limbs, was a thought that broke my courage.

Parthenia Hague, "save women and children and the negro slaves."[42]

Many women responded to the Northern troops by running away. These women loaded their families and their valuables onto carts and headed out for safety. Most of these women who sought refuge only took along foodstuffs, clothing, and silverware. But some women did their best to move their entire households. One South Carolina woman packed all her parlor furniture—including her beloved piano.

These women had different destinations. Some, expecting the Union troops to pass by quickly, hid in nearby forests and swamps until they could return safely to their homes. Others headed for the homes of relatives in nearby towns. Still, many refugees had no particular place to go. Moving from one over-priced boarding house to another, these displaced women bartered their possessions for food, watched their remaining money dwindle, and waited for the end of the war. Conditions for the refugees were usually dismal indeed. "We tried to eat without seeing or tasting [and] to sleep without touching the bed," wrote Kate Stone of her escape into Texas. "We certainly had found the dark corner of the Confederacy."[43]

The problem of the refugees came to a head with the advance of General William

Some Southern women piled their families and valuables onto carts and fled to safety ahead of advancing Union armies.

Women of the Civil War

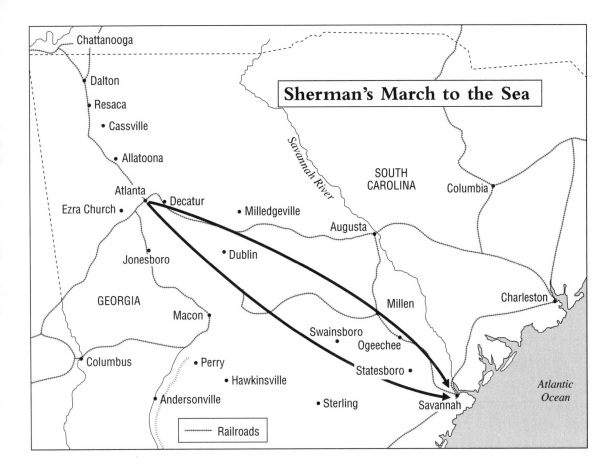

Sherman's March to the Sea

Chattanooga
Dalton
Resaca
Cassville
Allatoona
Atlanta
Ezra Church
Decatur
Milledgeville
Jonesboro
Dublin
SOUTH CAROLINA
Columbia
Savannah River
Augusta
GEORGIA
Macon
Millen
Charleston
Swainsboro
Ogeechee
Columbus
Perry
Statesboro
Hawkinsville
Andersonville
Sterling
Savannah
Atlantic Ocean

········· Railroads

Tecumseh Sherman across Georgia and the Carolinas in 1864–1865. Sherman's army created a wide swath of destruction. Anticipating Sherman's ruthless attack, thousands of Confederate women fled their homes as the Union troops neared. Many waited until the last minute, hoping that the troops would change course. "We only saved our clothes," wrote the wife of a Confederate general. "How fortunate we were to do that for many saved nothing. We left with the roar of the cannon in our ears!"[44]

"Like Demons They Rush In"

Still, many women chose not to flee when the Union soldiers came near. For some, this decision was based on the reality that there was no guarantee of safety elsewhere or simply no means of getting away. Others held out hope that they could convince the Northerners to leave them alone. And still others resolved to stand and defend what little they had, no matter what. Having lost so much else in the war, they could not see abandoning what remained.

Anticipating danger, these women took precautions, of course. Many buried their silverware and jewelry to hide them from the soldiers. They also concealed what food they had not yet eaten. Some hid their remaining bacon at the bottom of trash heaps. A North Carolina woman stowed sacks of flour under her bed. Occasionally the strategy worked. More often, it did not. Northern soldiers, accustomed to the game, searched relentlessly through houses and dug up yards while the women watched in anger and despair.

But women who left their valuables in the open fared no better. "Like demons they rush in," wrote a Georgia woman about Sherman's troops. "To my smoke-house, my dairy, pantry, kitchen, and cellar, like famished wolves they come, breaking locks and whatever is in their way."[45] Soldiers helped themselves to jewelry and took away old plow horses; they put silver serving dishes in their knapsacks and marched off with most of the women's remaining food. The troops routinely burned houses, fields, and entire towns when they were ready to move on.

The purpose of Sherman's march was to break the back of the Confederacy, and it succeeded. Sherman left a wake of destruction from which the South could not recover. Many of the women who suffered from his soldiers' heavy-handed tactics deeply resented the invasion and continued to hold out hope that the Confederacy could survive. But by the time the troops had passed, most of these women knew that such a hope was in vain.

Years of shortages, separations, and Yankee occupation had taken their toll. The war was no longer about patriotic ideas and nationalistic fervor. All but the most intensely anti-Union women could now agree that a different principle was at stake. "Do you know what you are fighting for?" a member of Sherman's army mockingly asked a North Carolina woman after the arrival of Union troops. Knowing that her food was nearly gone, that her furnishings had been destroyed, and that many of her family heirlooms were now in the hands of the Yankees, she did not hesitate in her answer. "Existence,"[46] she told him.

Chapter 3:
Nurses

While most women stayed in their home communities during the Civil War, a significant minority did not. Those who left their homes did so for several reasons. Among the most important of these was to serve as a nurse. The thousands of women on both sides who chose this job offered compassion, hope, and practical care to sick and injured soldiers. They brought knowledge, hard work, and courage to their task, and their intervention often meant the difference between life and death for the troops. "God knows what we should have done without them," remarked a Union official about the nurses who served the North. "They have worked like heroes night and day."[47]

Accurate statistics on the number of women who worked as Civil War nurses are difficult to come by. Not only was record keeping inconsistent, but there was no central authority in charge of all nurses. Some nurses were hired and supervised more or less directly by their governments. Many more independently volunteered their time and services, and still others were part of a variety of private organizations active in relief work. In all, historians estimate that up to twenty thousand women served as nurses for the Union alone, with a number nearly as high for the Confederacy; and this figure does not count women who served briefly and informally as the need arose.

Primitive Medical Care

The need for nurses was great. The Civil War was an extremely bloody conflict. The total number of casualties in the Civil War was greater than in all other wars in the nation's history combined. By the mid-1800s, advances in technology brought on by the Industrial Revolution had made weapons more accurate, powerful, and lethal than they had been during earlier American wars. Thus, Civil War wounds tended to be both numerous and serious, requiring immediate medical attention.

Moreover, those who escaped wounds on the battlefield often could not escape disease. Unsanitary conditions, poor diet and hygiene, exposure to the elements, and the close quarters in which the soldiers lived all created a breeding ground for infectious diseases such as smallpox, tuberculosis, and the intestinal disorders of cholera and dysentery. Many of these illnesses were killers. Indeed, more than half of the war's dead succumbed to disease rather than to wounds. Even those who survived the illnesses were often in desperate need of extended medical care.

At the same time, medical technology was still in its infancy. Sanitary standards and sterilization techniques were nonexistent in field hospitals and surgeries. X rays and antibiotics were unknown. Medical personnel frequently used ether and chloroform to ease patients' pain, but these early anesthetics were not well understood and were often not used safely and effectively. To save as many lives as efficiently as possible, amputation was the standard treatment for most leg and arm wounds. Only a few doctors of the time opposed this practice; among them, it is interesting to note, was a woman, Mary Walker, who was one of a handful of female doctors practicing during the war.

Dr. Mary Walker was one of a handful of women who practiced medicine in the army during the Civil War.

Women's Work?

The combination of rampant disease, increased firepower, and a limited professional medical corps led to an enormous demand for nurses. In some ways, this demand provided a perfect opportunity for a patriotic and compassionate woman to help her cause. While polite society frowned on women taking on work outside the home, the rules were somewhat less strict when it came to nursing. Mothers, after all, nursed their children through illness, and wives cared for their husbands when they were sick. To some observers, hospital and battlefield nursing seemed a reasonable extension of traditional gender roles for women.

The role of nurses in a recent European conflict gave this argument particular strength. During the Crimean War of the 1840s, a young Englishwoman named Florence Nightingale had volunteered her services as a nurse. Overcoming objections from her parents and from many in the British medical community, she had worked tirelessly to help ill and wounded soldiers. Nightingale had also built an organization of nurses and encouraged other women to join her service. To those who championed the work of female nurses, Nightingale was a wonderful example of what women could accomplish.

But others sharply disagreed. A few observers believed that women were too unpredictable to work in a setting where they must take orders. They argued that male nurses would better accept the authority of higher-ranking doctors. According to this perspective, the problem was not so much a lack of medical knowledge on the part of women but an inability to recognize and accept their "place." "When [female nurses] presume to direct or control the physician," warned one newspaper editor, "their services may well be dispensed with."[48]

Other dissenters objected to women nurses on different grounds. In their view, there was something not quite seemly about a woman engaging in wartime service. A calm and peaceful sickroom in a fine home was one thing; a grimy hospital full of bleeding, vomiting soldiers was another. The heavy lifting, the long hours, and the stress of dealing with terrible wounds would surely prove too much for American womanhood; or so many Americans on both sides believed.

But attitudes shifted as the demand for nurses grew. As pioneering nurse Clara Barton put it, while military nursing could indeed be "rough and unseemly for a *woman*," fighting was just as "rough and unseemly for *men*."[49] While some men did serve as nurses, it soon became evident that able-bodied men were better used as soldiers. Moreover, it seemed to some people that women were superior at the job. One Confederate study suggested that female nurses were twice as effective as their male counterparts in healing the wounded. Enthusiastically in some cases and reluctantly in others, the medical establishment began to take on women as nurses—and occasionally as hospital administrators as well.

"It Was a Necessity"

Nevertheless, there remained serious questions about what sort of woman would make a good nurse. Some observers argued that only single women should serve, as a married woman's place was squarely in the home and in the service of

Clara Barton

Union nurse Clara Barton was one of the most famous women to take part in the Civil War. Born in 1821, she was the youngest of five siblings; she was so much younger than the rest, in fact, that she liked to say that she grew up with six parents. When she was eleven, one of her brothers became seriously ill. Young Clara took an active role in nursing him back to health—a process that took two years. However, in the years before the Civil War she spent most of her time teaching school, doing various kinds of charitable work, and serving as a clerk in the national patent office.

The Civil War changed Barton's life. Aware that Union soldiers needed plenty of medical attention, she threw herself wholeheartedly into nursing. She remained independent of the federal government throughout the war, relying mainly on private donations for the supplies and equipment she would need. But she also talked federal officials into allowing her the use of government wagons, mule teams, and spare food when her own supplies ran low. Her most important nursing services took place in 1862, when she personally served at the battles of Fredericksburg, Antietam, Chantilly, Second Bull Run, and others.

Barton also played an important role at the end of the war. In 1865 she established an office that listed Union soldiers who were officially missing in action. Some had been killed on the battlefield, and others were deserters; but many more had been taken prisoner. Barton supervised efforts to locate as many of these men as possible and report their status to families. After the war, she helped organize the marking of Union graves at the Confederacy's notorious Andersonville prison camp.

Barton is best known, though, for a task she took on many years after the end of the war. During a trip to Europe, she became interested in the International Red Cross—a neutral group dedicated to easing the sufferings of wounded soldiers and victims of disasters. In 1877, she began to organize an American affiliate. Although most Americans were not terribly interested in the idea at first, Barton persevered. She founded the American Red Cross in 1881, and devoted most of her energies to that group until her resignation as the organization's president in 1904—eight years before her death.

her husband. Others, fearing romances between nurses and patients and the loss of nurses to marriage, advocated the opposite. Social reformer Dorothea Dix, who served as the Union's foremost nursing administrator, had especially strong notions on the subject. "No woman under thirty years need apply to serve in government hospitals," she wrote in an appeal for women to come forward and serve. "All nurses are required to be very plain-looking women."[50]

Despite these concerns, however, women of all ages and all walks of life

A nurse in a Union army hospital writes a letter home for a wounded soldier.

served as military nurses. Twenty-three-year-old Cornelia Hancock of New Jersey was one of many young women who defied Dix's orders. More typical was Union nurse "Mother" Mary Ann Bickerdyke, who was in her midforties, but married, single, and widowed women of all ages volunteered their services. A few nurses who were mothers brought their children with them when they signed up for the job.

The women did not all share the same motivations for serving. For some, the primary goal was idealistic. Many of these women felt a patriotic impulse to help their country in any capacity possible. In particular, some felt deep compassion for the soldiers on the battlefield. "I've longed to be a man," wrote the novelist Louisa May Alcott, who was disappointed that women were barred from enlisting in the army. "But as I can't fight I will content myself with working for those who can."[51]

Many nurses, though, were less idealistic. Some simply wanted to escape the humdrum routines of their hometowns. A few of these saw nursing as an opportunity to travel. That was especially tempting in a time when people rarely ventured more than a hundred miles from home. Many of the women who served as nurses were leaving their home state for the first time, and a few had never left their home county.

The issue of money was important, too. Dorothea Dix had requested that nurses be women of independent means, but this was not always the case. Women whose men had gone to war often found themselves on the brink of poverty. Since most nursing positions offered a small salary, usually about twelve dollars a month, the job could help women make ends meet. "The choice of such a life would naturally be an absurdity," wrote a formerly well-off woman in answer to the question of why she became a nurse. But, she continued, "I had no means and it was a necessity."[52]

Hospitals, Battlegrounds, and Training

Most women who signed up to nurse were quickly shipped to one of two places. The majority were sent to hospitals at a safe distance from the fighting. These facilities, known as general, or brigade, hospitals, varied considerably. Some general hospitals were little more than tents, while others were converted schools, town halls, or hotels. The Union nurses, in particular, often worked aboard so-called hospital ships—boats moored in rivers or bays not far from the fighting. All these hospitals served soldiers who had become sick or who had been wounded in battle.

Other women were shipped directly to field hospitals, which were as close as practicable to the battlegrounds. Most of these battlefield nurses worked behind the lines, tending to wounded soldiers as their fellow troops brought them in. Once the fighting was over, they ventured out onto the battleground in search of other injured men. However, Clara Barton—among the most famous nurses of the war and the eventual founder of the American Red Cross—was an exception to this rule. "I did not wait for

American Red Cross founder Clara Barton obtained and distributed medical supplies during the Civil War.

reporters and journalists to tell us that a battle had been fought," she said. "I went in while the battle raged"[53]—and she helped assist the soldiers as the bullets sailed around her.

Whether they served far from the battlefield or amid the fighting, most women received very little formal training. In part, this was a result of the demand for nurses. Administrators were in a hurry to get women into the field as quickly as they could, and taking time for training simply slowed that process. Cornelia Hancock, for example, signed up for duty as soon as the news of the Battle of Gettysburg reached Philadelphia. Within three days, she had arrived at the battleground.

Popular stereotypes about women also played a role in the general lack of instruction. Women were widely viewed as nurturing, compassionate, and virtuous. Even people who disapproved of women serving in hospitals agreed with the general perspective that women had an innate talent for nursing. As a result, men and women alike believed that women would instinctively know how to handle a suffering patient. As one female hospital administrator described it, nursing represented "woman's true sphere."[54]

True sphere or not, training would have been a wise strategy. Some of the women who worked as nurses completely lacked nursing skills. Many soldiers served as unfortunate guinea pigs to women who had to teach themselves to change dressings or bandage wounds. Even less pleasant stories abounded of women who offered rich foods to patients with terrible abdominal disorders. Other tales told of eager young nurses who loosened the dressings on men's wounds, hoping to make them more comfortable; unfortunately, the men quickly bled to death.

Turned Stomachs and Gruesome Sights

Training would have been helpful in another way, too. Most of the women who entered the hospitals and the battlefields were wholly unprepared for the horrors they would see. The smells of decaying flesh, the sounds of screaming soldiers, and the sights of amputated limbs and spurting blood were all enough to overwhelm the strongest and most dedicated of nurses. While some bravely continued to serve, a number of nurses quickly decided they were not suited for the work.

In some cases, in fact, even the most straightforward of hospital tasks proved too much for the would-be nurses. "The surgeon asked me if I would wash [a patient's] wound," reported Cornelia McDonald of Virginia, who was hoping to be of help in a Confederate hospital. "I

Women Doctors

❧

The first American woman doctor was Elizabeth Blackwell. Born in England in 1821, Blackwell emigrated to the United States while a child. She was determined to earn a medical degree, but nearly every school she applied to turned her down because she was a woman. Finally, Geneva College in New York State accepted her. It turned out the college meant the acceptance as a joke, but Blackwell took her place and completed her degree.

Although Blackwell was not directly involved in caring for patients during the war, she played several roles in the conflict. More than almost anyone else, she spoke up for the systematic training of nurses. She even started a small New York school which taught young women the basics of the job, although the school turned out only a handful of Civil War nurses. She was considered for the post of Union nursing supervisor, too, a job which ultimately went to the social reformer Dorothea Dix; and she was active in the founding of the New York Central Association of Relief, a Union aid society.

Of women who served in the war as physicians, the most notable was Mary Walker, who was born in 1832 in Oswego, New York. After trying in vain to get an appointment as a surgeon in the Union army, Walker served as a volunteer in a Washington hospital. Later, she went to battlefields and did medical work near Fredericksburg, Virginia. In 1863, she traveled to Tennessee, where she was at last given the job of assistant surgeon over the objections of both War Department officials and men in the ranks.

Wearing an officer's uniform, Walker worked with civilians and soldiers alike. At one point she was captured by the Confederates and held prisoner for several months. However, Walker did not last long in the service. While she was in many ways an excellent physician, she was abrasive and somewhat eccentric, and she was quietly dropped from the Union army's medical staff early in 1865.

tried to say yes, but the thought of it made me so faint that I could only stagger towards the door."[55] For a few, even walking into a hospital was more than they could bear.

Some who could not stomach direct medical care did return for occasional visits to recuperation wards, where they read aloud to patients or washed the faces of the less seriously injured. This sort of work did make life easier for some of the patient, but only up to a point. A cartoon of the time showed a genteel woman asking a soldier if she could sponge off his face for him. "You may if you want to very bad," replied the soldier, "but you'll be the fourteenth lady as has done it this blessed morning."[56] The more sturdy nurses dismissed these women visitors as "picknickers" who lacked the courage to venture from "the clean, sweet, and fresh wards."[57]

While a few of these women might not have been able to manage the demands of nursing under any circumstances, it is likely that some would have done quite well if they had been given a gradual and compassionate introduction to the job. But medical and governmental leaders never established a more thorough training program during the war. The idea that nursing was woman's true sphere was too strong, and the need for nurses was too great. Training was poor at the start of the war, poor in the middle of the war, and poor at the end of the war. Women who wanted to nurse got very little help in preparing themselves for the ordeal that lay ahead.

"We'll Help You All We Can"

However, many women were able to acclimate themselves to the hospital and to the battlefields. For the most part, they squarely faced the horrors that surrounded them; the disgust and sorrow they experienced spurred them on to a higher level of compassionate care. Far from becoming immune to the suffering, their recognition of its power gave them strength in fighting against it. "The very sight of his face is distressing," wrote Confederate nurse and hospital administrator Kate Cumming about one wounded soldier, "and makes me feel as if I would sacrifice almost any thing to palliate [ease] his pain."[58]

Many Union nurses shared Cumming's feelings. Annie Wittenmyer, for example, reported watching dead and wounded soldiers being unloaded into her hospital boat near Shiloh, Illinois. "At first we could only cover our faces with our hands in a shiver and chill of agony," she reported, "in the attempts to hide the horrid sights of war from our eyes." But when the wounded asked for food and drink, she and her fellow nurses responded. "I called out cheerily, 'Yes, yes; *we'll help you all we can*,'"[59] Wittenmyer recalled. She spent the rest of the day distributing food, water, and bandages in an effort to lighten the soldiers' suffering.

Still, nurses were so busy that they had little time to think consciously about the horrors that they saw. The days frequently became a steady succession of wounds to be dressed, medicines

Women volunteered by the thousands as nurses in army hospitals, but they were poorly trained and unprepared for the horrors they would encounter.

to be given, and men to be comforted. Most nurses were expected to work fourteen- to sixteen-hour days six days a week. Few hospitals were well staffed to begin with, and most suffered from a steady loss of nurses throughout the war, leaving even more work for those who stayed.

Responsibilities

The specific jobs of a nurse varied considerably from day to day and even from minute to minute. Many nurses had expected to be involved in medical care, and indeed nearly all nurses did change dressings and bandage wounds, with some helping out in operating rooms. But that was only the beginning of the typical nurse's responsibilities. "There are so few of us," sighed one administrator, "that our nurses must do anything and everything—make beds, wait upon anybody, and often half a dozen at a time."[60]

Anything and everything was exactly right. Nurses spent much of their time involved in all manner of activities that were not strictly medical. As one contemporary writer rather sentimentally described it, nurses could be found "wiping clammy foreheads, soothing feverish fancies, moistening parched lips, writing messages of love and hope to distant homes, singing hymns of Christian cheer, and closing the lids over glazing eyes."[61] In some cases, these roles were secondary to the women's medical work. In others, they were just as important.

Very often, too, filling these roles required a great deal of creativity. While a few hospitals had plenty of supplies, most did not. Nurses frequently tore up their old petticoats to serve as bandages, jury-rigged bedding from whatever was available, and did their best to feed hundreds of men with limited food, poor kitchens, and few cooking utensils. The deprivations were especially apparent on the battlefield. But nurses in hospitals were also forced to confront shortages, especially in the South.

The various tasks performed by the nurses were deeply appreciated by the patients themselves. Being wounded was a terrifying experience for a soldier. Not only were the men in pain, but most were far from home and family, and most were well aware of the high mortality rate following injury or infection. Under the circumstances, any comfort the women could offer was a considerable help, and the most skilled nurses were quite good at it. Nor did the nurses restrict their attentions to those who would live. For example, Union nurse Harriet Whetten gladly held the hand of a mortally wounded soldier so he would not have to die alone.

Many of the survivors, in fact, never forgot the women who had attended to them on the battlefield or in the hospital. Patients were usually overjoyed to leave the hospitals upon recovering, especially if they were being sent home; but they were often reluctant to leave the nurses who had taken such good care of them. Some nurses would later receive letters from soldiers thanking them for their individual kindnesses. "Hundreds of men, scattered all over the states, will always remember and revere her,"[62] wrote one soldier of Union nurse Mary Husband—and Husband was far from the only one who earned such praise.

Hardships and Joys

But while soldiers were glad to have nurses, doctors and government officials were not always so sure. Some doctors did their best to make life difficult for nurses. They screamed at the women and called them names; they expected nurses to carry out tasks they had not been ordered to do; they ignored sensible suggestions made by nurses simply because nurses had made them. Kate Cumming left one hospital for a new one because she saw she had no chance of ever pleasing the chief surgeon.

But some nurses returned this sort of treatment to doctors and to government officials alike. Women like Clara Barton and Dorothea Dix were not accustomed to waiting for orders. Nor were they inclined to ask permission before acting. If they saw a way of alleviating the sufferings of their patients, they would do it regardless of the consequences. As a result, many of these women ran into difficulties

"Giving You the Particulars"

An unknown number of Civil War women briefly took on nursing tasks when the battle came near their homes. These women often opened their houses to the wounded and did their best to make the young men comfortable. They also tried to notify family members if the soldiers died. This excerpt, quoted in *War Letters*, was written by Martha Liggan of Virginia to the mother of Confederate soldier O.H. Middleton:

I now seat myself to reply to your letter for the purpose of giving you the particulars concerning the death of your noble son, who was mortaly wounded here on 30th of May.

The ball struck the left arm between the shoulder and the elbow, entering the body [a] little below the arm pit [and] passing through the lungs, [coming] out under the left shoulder blade bone. . . . Your son was brought to the house about sun down, by my father and one of the Yankeys. They found him a very little distance from the house. It is supposed he had been lying there some time, for he was very near speechless, when they got him here. I bathed his wound, washed his face and hands. That revived him very much. He would raise his head from the pillow and speak very distinctly. . . .

Sometimes he was res[t]less, because we couldn't move him on the bed to ease him, his wound was so painful. . . . We asked the Yankeys to let us send for our family physician, they told us no they could not do that. Oh vile and unfeeling wretches, I hope they may receive [their] reward.

Mrs. Middleton could not have been pleased to hear this account of how the Union troops had treated her son. However, it is likely that she was grateful to Liggan for taking the time to inform her of the details of his death—and for doing her best to take care of the young man.

with politicians and bureaucrats over their tendency to make up their own rules.

The most notorious—and most effective—of these rulebreakers was Union nurse "Mother" Mary Ann Bickerdyke. Bickerdyke routinely commandeered shipments of supplies for use at her hospitals and ignored or intimidated doctors who tried to tell her what to do. Salty, uneducated, and blunt, Bickerdyke had no patience with those who stood in her way. Once a doctor angrily asked her where she had gotten the order to take supplies that had been earmarked for somewhere else. "From the Lord God Almighty," she shot back. "Do you have anything that ranks higher than that?"[63]

Nurses suffered other problems, too. Their sleeping quarters were often little more than rude cots in communal hospital rooms, although some—especially those who had brought their children along—did board with local families. Their food was standard army fare, if that: fatty bacon, hard biscuits, and whatever else was available. Many women became sick from the workload and from the germs and infections that ran rampant among the soldiers. Nurses missed their families, as well. Whether they had signed up for idealistic reasons or for money, hundreds of women became so homesick that they gave up their posts and returned home early.

But for those who persevered, the experience of nursing was well worth the struggle. Those who served came to see their work as a kind of sacred gift. They were engaged in the vital task of saving lives and comforting the wounded; and nothing seemed more important. "I feel almost for the first time in my life that I am of some use,"[64] mused Confederate nurse Ada Bacot. The satisfaction of a critical job done well was enough to make up for almost any kind of hardship.

Indeed, some women were surprised to find that nursing spoke to something deep inside them. In no other area of their existence had these nurses felt so sure of themselves, so satisfied with their work, or so fully connected to those around them. Many nurses often experienced a kind of exuberance that told them they were doing exactly the right thing. "We all know in our hearts that it is thorough enjoyment to be here," wrote Katharine Wormeley about her work aboard a Union hospital ship. "*It is life*, in short; and we wouldn't be anywhere else for anything in the world."[65]

Chapter 4:
Camp Women

Civil War army camps were populated overwhelmingly by men. Virtually all the officers and soldiers were men, of course, and most of the support staff at the camps consisted of men as well. The drummers, buglers, and fifers who summoned the soldiers for meals, drills, and roll calls were men, or in some cases teenage boys. The sutlers, peddlers who set up traveling stores in or near the camps, were nearly always men, too; and the army personnel in charge of supplies and deliveries were likewise predominantly male.

But a varied group of women followed an ancient military tradition and traveled with the soldiers from encampment to encampment. Sometimes known as "daughters of the regiment," camp followers, or vivandières, these women served as washerwomen or cooks, begged the soldiers for money, sold goods and services to the troops, or filled the ornamental role of mascot or cheerleader to the regiment. Whatever the role, the life

of a camp woman was a difficult and dangerous one, and the constant travel created many hardships. Still, for hundreds of women on both sides of the conflict, staying home seemed a good deal less appealing than following the troops.

Wives and Other Relatives

A large number of the women who followed the camps were relatives of the men who served. Most were wives of enlisted men and officers, although some mothers, sisters, and daughters traveled with the armies as well. These women knew perfectly well what the hardships of army travel would be, but they saw little point in remaining alone at home while their men went off to war. Despite the difficulties that would lie ahead, these women made the conscious decision to stay with their husbands.

For most, in fact, the decision was not particularly difficult. Staying at home meant a life of hardship and constant anxiety waiting for news from the front. In the case of women without close family ties in their villages and towns, too, staying at home often meant loneliness. A few women moved in with other relatives, but this was an unwelcome option for many. And some Confederate women, displaced by the fighting, had little choice but to come to their husbands. For women in these circumstances, traveling with the army meant making the best of a bad situation.

Being with the army could have other advantages, too. Although camp life could be boring and colorless, there was at least the possibility of excitement. Certainly the army offered more variety and intrigue than did the typical small town of the 1860s. The chance of adventure was a powerful motivator, just as it

Many women traveled with their soldier husbands during the Civil War and endured primitive camp conditions.

was for many women who enlisted as nurses. And for those women who suspected that their men would gamble, drink, or otherwise misbehave, being close to the troops offered them the opportunity to monitor their husbands.

Still, the most common reason that wives and other relatives traveled with the army was their desire to be with the men they loved. Of course, the women could not usually accompany their husbands into battle; but under the best of circumstances it was possible for couples to spend plenty of time together. "When the forces are in garrison," wrote a contemporary observer, "she [that is, the wife of a soldier] can be with him constantly."[66] Constantly was an exaggeration; camp soldiers had a long and rather dreary list of duties that would have interfered with perpetual togetherness. However, that promise of companionship was a great comfort to women who wanted to travel with the armies.

The Men's Reactions

Some of the soldiers felt exactly as their women did. "My husband was anxious to have me accompany him,"[67] recalled Belle Reynolds of Peoria, Illinois. Many of these men feared loneliness just as their wives did. They longed for the presence of the women they loved, hoping to make the hardships of soldier life somewhat easier to bear. For the male half of many couples, the idea of being apart from their wives for weeks, months, or perhaps even years was inconceivable.

But not all men wanted their wives around. In some cases, the men were deeply concerned with questions of propriety. Camp could be a rough place. Just as people often believed that nursing was no job for a lady, so too did many men believe that army life would corrupt and offend their women. Mary Logan, for instance, wanted to live with her husband, John, at the Union encampment. But John, a Union general, feared that his wife would be the subject of damaging gossip if she stayed at the camp for even an occasional visit. "Don't come any more to camp," he wrote in a blunt letter of 1862. "I will meet you in Cairo [Illinois] or come home when I can."[68]

John Logan's concerns were legitimate. Camp women were often subject to insults and abuse from men who resented their presence. A woman in camp without a male relative at hand was an especially appealing target, but married women were not exempt from gossip and innuendo. Rumors swirled around camps, for instance, claiming that certain women had been seen flirting with men who were not their husbands—a serious offense in a strongly moralistic time. Some of these women may indeed have been flirting, but others were simply the victims of misinterpretations or malicious lies.

Some women, too, were the target of rough and teasing practical jokes. Many of the victims, though, were hardly the type to submit meekly, as indicated by this soldier's description of an incident involving a camp woman known as "Dutch Mary":

One private, thinking to have a little sport at her expense, once came up behind her as she was washing some clothes at the brook, and kissed her. She seized a wet shirt and belabored him right and left, pursuing him out of camp, to the great amusement of his comrades and chagrin of himself. When next he felt in a jocose frame of mind, no doubt he didn't take Dutch Mary as the object of his mirth.[69]

Men sometimes advised their wives to stay apart to avoid the risk of pregnancy. During the war, many couples put off having more children. Pregnancy and childbirth, moreover, were difficult enough under the best of circumstances, and the

The Good Life in an Army Camp

Most army encampments were rather grim and spartan places. However, when armies stayed in one place for some time, it became possible to build more substantial shelters and to create more welcoming surroundings. In a few places, camps became much more luxurious places than most soldiers would have thought possible. That was particularly true during the winter, when the fighting quieted temporarily and men dug themselves in for the poor weather.

Often, the winters were times when young ladies who lived nearby would come and visit the unmarried officers; they were also times when married officers were most likely to summon their wives. In some camps, the presence of women served as an excuse to hold feasts, fancy balls, and concerts. The women who attended the festivities given at the winter camps of the Union's Army of the Potomac were delighted with the quality of the food, the extravagance of the entertainment, and—perhaps most of all—the officer-to-woman ratio of about four to one. While balls and feasts were not standard fare for camp women, they were routine experiences for a select and lucky few.

hardships of camp life made both more complicated still. The wife of General Dorsey Pender became pregnant three times during the war, much to her dismay. Pender, however, blamed her for the pregnancies, pointing out that she had chosen to come to camp with him. "Surely if you do not want children you will have to remain away from me,"[70] Pender told her reproachfully.

Officially, too, the armies were not well disposed to the notion of women accompanying their men. A few generals did not object when their officers brought along family members. But most were less than delighted with the prospect. In their view, women were distractions. Their presence could take the soldiers' minds off their duties and slow a unit on the move. Moreover, having women nearby meant that valuable time and energy might have to be expended in protecting and defending them.

As a result, women often encountered official barriers if they wanted to accompany their men. Wives who asked permission from their husbands' commanding officers usually were turned down. Some, anticipating refusal, did not even try. Confederate general Jubal Early summed up the prevailing army attitude toward women in his comment about fellow general John Gordon's wife, who spent much of the war following her husband from camp to camp: "I wish the Yankees would capture Mrs. Gordon and hold her till the war was over."[71]

But in fact, most generals had little ability to control the flow of wives and other relatives in and out of the camps. They were too concerned with matters of strategy and supplies to worry overmuch about the presence of women. Knowing this, many women did not bother to ask permission to accompany their men. Instead, they informally joined the regiment and, in effect, dared the authorities to evict them. Once in, these determined women proved extremely difficult to get out. One Tennessee woman fell into a routine in which she would be driven out of camp and then sneak back in a few days later. Many others did just the same.

Washerwomen and Cooks

To be sure, even commanders like Jubal Early recognized the usefulness of some women in camp. Chief on this list were women who served the army in some very exhausting and low-paying jobs usually scorned by men. Union regiments, for instance, traveled with washerwomen, who kept the soldiers' clothing as clean as possible. The work involved lifting piles of heavy clothes, stooping over tubs of boiling water, and scrubbing out stains and sweat with abrasive soaps that irritated the hands.

Women of the Civil War

This washerwoman (left), with her children, found low-paying but steady work with the Union army.

Other women served the regiments as cooks. Soldiers were more likely to take on this role than they were to do laundry, but regiments tended to prefer the cooking of women. Besides, hiring a woman to do the job freed men for more traditional soldier activities. Like doing the laundry, cooking was a tiring experience. It was also frustrating. Women had to make do with whatever food supplies they were given, many of which—especially among the Confederate armies—turned out to be rancid or full of bugs; and the typical camp did not provide much in the way of kitchen equipment or storage space.

Most cooks and washerwomen were wives or other relatives of the soldiers. Nearly all came from the lower classes. The work they were assigned was hard, but most women who served in these roles were used to hard work and would return to menial work in civilian life. And while the pay was low, these women were accustomed to low wages. Indeed, because the armies offered them steady work, these women could often make more money at the camps than they could by staying at home.

Daughters of the Regiment

One distinctive nonpaying position open to women in both armies was the so-called daughter of the regiment. In essence, the women who served in this role were ornaments: They dressed in quasi-military garb, carried flags during parades and occasional drills, and exhorted the troops to fight bravely. Most of these women were wives of young soldiers, though occasionally someone's daughter or sister would fill the role instead. As historian Agatha Young describes her, the daughter of the regiment "was supposed to have style, in a pert, drum-majorette sort of way."[72]

The women who served in this capacity were indeed stylish. "A more jaunty or bewitching little Daughter of the Regiment never handled the can-

Women Entertainers

Ladies from nearby communities often came to army camps to sing and recite poetry for the soldiers and the officers. Jenny Cary and Hetty Cary, for example, were Richmond sisters who often visited the Confederate Army of Northern Virginia. Their musical repertoire included the Confederate song "Maryland, My Maryland!" an appeal to the government of that state to join the secession movement; while their audience appreciated all their selections, they usually found "Maryland, My Maryland!" the highlight of the evening.

Among the Northern counterparts to the Cary sisters was Elida Rumsey Fowle. She had wanted to be a nurse but was rejected by Dorothea Dix because she was not yet twenty when she applied. That was probably just as well; she apparently could not stand the sight of blood. Instead, she entertained the troops by singing them popular songs. In one year she gave at least two hundred concerts in the camps and at the front. She was especially noteworthy because she sang while standing on a Confederate flag, on which, at especially dramatic points in the music, she would stamp her feet.

teen," wrote an observer about Hanna Ewbank of Wisconsin. Ewbank's uniform was certainly ornate; according to the observer, it included a jacket "trimmed with military buttons and gold lace," a scarlet skirt, a pair of fancy boots, and a "hat of blue velvet trimmed with white and gold lace, with yellow plumes."[73] And Ewbank was just one of many regimental daughters who wore similar outfits.

The daughters of the regiment were generally liked and respected by the soldiers they served. They were personable young women, and their encouraging attitude was an inspiration to many. "Never pouting," a Union soldier wrote admiringly about another Wisconsin daughter of the regiment, Eliza Wilson; "with a kind word for every one, and every one a kind word for her."[74] However, any misstep could cause a regimental daughter to fall out of favor. One Confederate private wrote scathingly of his regiment's mascot, whom he had seen drinking. "A drunken man is bad enough," he complained, "but a drunken woman is a dreadful sight."[75]

Sutlers, Beggars, and Prostitutes

The daughters of the regiment served without any pay at all, and the cooks and washerwomen received very little. But some of the women who followed the troops could make a very comfortable living. These were the sutlers. Sutlers purchased cloth, food, and other items in towns and cities at relatively low cost and transported them to the camps and battlefields, where they sold them to the troops at outrageously high prices. Sutlers were known for driving hard bargains and for rarely giving an inch to soldiers who complained of the expense. As one contemporary observer put it, "the only place a sutler could find sympathy was in the dictionary."[76]

Although most of the sutlers were men, some were husband-and-wife teams, and a few were women who worked alone. Among those in the latter category was Marie Tebe, sometimes known as Mary Tippee. When Tebe's husband joined a Pennsylvania regiment, she came with him and began service as a sutler. Her husband, however, disapproved of Tebe's presence. Hoping to push her to return home, he conspired with some of his friends to steal most of the money she had made. Undaunted, Tebe did not give up sutlering; she simply moved on to another regiment.

Female sutlers were less common, though, than lower-class women who followed the troops out of perceived necessity. Most of these women had led difficult lives. Extremely poor and generally uneducated, they hoped that the soldiers could help improve their condition.

Most camps, for instance, had beggar women, often old or sick, to whom the more kindhearted soldiers might give a few coins or an extra blanket when they had the means.

Other women tried to make a living by selling goods and services that were somewhat less legal than those provided by the sutlers. Some women smuggled bottles of bootleg whiskey into the camps, especially into camps in which alcohol was officially forbidden. The big skirts popular at the time helped conceal the jugs the women carried. One woman was famous for bringing five gallons of illegal alcohol into an encampment on every visit from town.

By all accounts, prostitution was commonplace in or around every good-sized army camp. As long as prostitutes did not create problems, some commanders tolerated their business, but other officers disapproved of the women's presence on moral and religious grounds. They also noted that prostitution could spread sexually transmitted diseases, which were difficult to cure and usually caused soldiers to spend time on sick leave.

Some prostitutes and beggars were also thieves. Upon returning to his tent after duty, more than one soldier discovered that his money, jewelry, or other valuables were missing. Sometimes the thieves were men, sometimes even the victim's fellow soldiers. But the record shows that many of the thieves were women. For those in enough need, even a handful of pennies or a small supply of dried meat could make a major difference. As a result, women who looked poor were sometimes viewed with deep suspicion by the men and officers alike.

Marie Tebe was a successful Civil War sutler, peddling goods to the Union troops.

Women of the Civil War

Camp Life

Official army accommodations were spartan at best and available only to washerwomen, cooks, and a few soldiers' wives. The officers' wives typically stayed in their husbands' quarters, which were separate from the tents and barracks where the enlisted men slept. Even so, the makeshift housing represented a rude shock for women of genteel backgrounds. Accustomed to servants, privacy, and warm beds, some had great trouble accepting the lack of luxuries on the march and in the encampments.

Other camp followers had limited housing choices, most of them unappealing. Occasionally an army might camp for a while very close to a good-sized town where rooms could be rented. But the women who followed the camps were generally forced to make do any way they could. Most wound up in squalid tent settlements that sprang up on the outskirts of the encampments, and some, like Bridget Divers of Michigan, usually slept in the open without even a tent.

Nearly all women agreed that the living conditions in and around the camps were harsh. As Belle Reynolds put it upon arriving at camp for the first time, "How could I stay in such a cheerless place? No floors, no chairs, the narrow cot my seat . . . the confusion of camp close around me, with but the thickness of cloth [that is, a tent] between me and the eyes of all, the scorching August sun streaming through the low-roofed covering—it seemed almost too much to endure."[77] Reynolds was relatively lucky. Taking pity on her, her husband's commander had her moved to a nearby boat, where the accommodations were a little more to her liking.

Food was no easier to accept. Few women of the time could be said to eat well, but those in the camps ate worse than many. In an era without refrigeration and with only a sketchy understanding of how to preserve food through canning, women ate what was available and hoped it had not gone bad. If they were there in an official capacity, the women of the camps usually ate the same monotonous and rather tasteless food offered to the soldiers. If they were there unofficially, they ate whatever scraps they could beg, buy, or steal.

Traveling with the armies was likewise difficult. The troops marched whenever the summons came, and they did so in all sorts of weather. Sometimes the women came along on foot—a harder task for them than for the men, given that women of the nineteenth century typically wore several layers of skirts, restrictive corsets, and shoes not designed for marching. Luckier, or perhaps wealthier, women rode in carriages or in horse-drawn ambulances instead of marching. Still, the cold, the heat, and the rain all made the women as uncomfortable as the men.

A very few women, primarily the wives of high-ranking officers, did enjoy a level of comfort at the camps not far from the standard to which they had been accustomed. One of the more unusual housing units during the war belonged to Agnes Salm-Salm, a Russian princess whose adventurer husband served for a time in the Union army. Salm-Salm had a carpeted tent complete with canopy bed, couch, and a separate bedroom for her maid; the food she was served, she said, was as good as anything she had eaten in Europe.

Nurses and Half Soldiers

The women who followed the troops often took on special responsibilities as the need for services arose. During battles, for instance, it was common for women to be pressed into service as water carriers, charged with bringing fresh water from nearby streams to the men in the field. Many were asked to sew as well, and most women who were anywhere nearby were expected to step in and nurse wounded soldiers as the need arose. Indeed, it often proved difficult to tell the nurses from the camp followers.

These extra duties were especially common among the cooks, the washer-women, and the daughters of the regiment—those with officially sanctioned roles. For some women, these extra demands proved too much, and they left the army as soon as they could. Others, though, counted it a privilege to serve in any way possible. In fact, many of the women in the camps longed to contribute to the cause in more tangible ways. They appreciated the chance to help out on the battlefield, and they did their best to get as close to the action as possible.

A few women got even closer to the battlefield while carrying water and nursing the wounded. Although these camp women did not take a regular uniformed part in the fighting, they were often described as half soldiers. The name fit. Kady Brownell, a Rhode Island daughter of the regiment, was one of several camp women who became famous for her heroics on the battlefield. At Bull Run, for example, Brownell was chosen to carry her regiment's flag onto the battleground. Once on the field, a contemporary reported, Brownell stayed put, giving the men a reference point even while the shooting was at its worst. "There she stood," added the writer with evident admiration, "unmoved and dauntless."[78]

Brownell was scarcely the only camp woman who sought out the action of the battlefield. Many came quite close to the fighting in their roles as water carriers, nurses, or cheerleaders. Bridget Divers "was a fearless and skillful rider," said an observer, "and as brave as the bravest under fire."[79] She often accompanied a cavalry unit into battle, offering support to the soldiers and first aid to the wounded. Despite a constant burst of shells, Rose Quinn Rooney of Louisiana pulled down a fence on a battlefield to let a group of Confederate soldiers pass through. And

Marie Tebe was noted for ignoring rifle fire in her zeal to provide the soldiers of her regiment with water. "Her skirts were riddled with bullets,"[80] wrote one soldier; but Tebe was not cowed.

Differences and Similarities

The camp women had many different reasons for following the troops. Like the nurses, they came from all walks of life and

Annie Etheridge

One of the best-known of the "half-soldier" women of the war was Annie Etheridge. Born in Michigan about 1840, she spent virtually all of the war as a daughter of the regiment for various units from her home state. Even the desertion of her soldier husband did not deter her from carrying out her duties. Contemporary accounts place her on the battlefields of Antietam, Second Bull Run, Gettysburg, Chancellorsville, and many more. She was popular and admired by the troops, as indicated by this account from a Maine soldier, quoted in Elizabeth D. Leonard's *All the Daring of a Soldier*:

Commenced to rise about daylight, and the first thing that greeted our optics was a female rising up from the

ground. It was none other than that heroine of the War, Annie Ether[i]dge, and a braver soul cannot be found. She is always on hand and ready to bear the same privations as the men. When danger threatens, she never cringes. At the battle of Fredericksburg she was binding the wounds of a man when a shell exploded nearby, tearing him terribly, and removing a large portion of the skirt of her dress. This morning she was surrounded by soldiers on every side, laying outside with no covering but her blanket, but her lodgings must have been selected voluntarily, for there isn't a man at any of the headquarters who wouldn't gladly surrender his bed and tent to her.

Officers' wives relax in relative comfort while visiting their husbands' camp. Enlisted men's wives experienced much harsher conditions.

all economic backgrounds. Some were motivated by patriotism, others by money. Some helped their nation's cause with battlefield heroics; others worked for the same goal through more mundane activities. Many camp women, especially the beggars, the prostitutes, and the thieves, made dubious contributions at best.

Similarly, the effect of their camp experiences on the members of each of these groups varied considerably. For most of the soldiers' wives, for instance, the struggle of managing camp life proved well worth the opportunity to spend time with their husbands. For the boldest of the half soldiers, the adventure of the battlefield offered a chance to break out of traditional women's roles. Indeed, Bridget Divers was so satisfied with her battleground experiences that she headed west after the war to take up a similar role among the soldiers fighting the Native Americans. And for the poorest women who populated the camps as beggars or prostitutes, life at the camps offered simple survival.

Chapter 5:
Women Spies, Militias, and Soldiers

❦

The most dramatic role switching during the Civil War was not that of women who became plantation managers, or political thinkers, or even "half soldiers" who carried water and rallied the troops on the battlefield. The ultimate "man's job" in wartime was combat, and in the Civil War a few women moved eagerly into that role. Some of these women served their armies as spies, scouts, and saboteurs, while others took on the task of defending their communities from invasion. And a surprising number of nineteenth-century women went even further. Disguising themselves as men, they secretly joined the armies and fought with a zeal that matched that of their male comrades.

Spies

One important way in which women served both the Union and Confederate armies was as spies. Probably thousands of women on both sides successfully passed on information to military officials at some point during the conflict. Most of these women, though, spied only occasionally and as the opportunity arose. Lola Sanchez of Florida, for example, once was

Confederate spy Belle Boyd was successful in part because Union officers spoke freely in front of her, assuming that no woman was capable of being a spy.

an unwilling host to two Union soldiers who came to her door and requested food. As they ate, they began discussing plans for an upcoming raid. Sanchez listened carefully; then she hurried through swamps and forest to bring the news to Confederate commanders.

But some women acted as full-time spies. By pretending to be something they were not, these women were able to pass on information on a regular basis. Confederate spy Belle Boyd, for instance, who was noted for her beauty, routinely flirted with Union soldiers. Charmed by her interest and perhaps more than a little naive, these soldiers were only too happy to respond to her wide-eyed questions about their work. In this way Boyd learned plenty about Union weapons, troop movements, and military weaknesses, all of which she immediately wrote down and sent via messenger to Confederate officials.

Union leaders were very slow to recognize Boyd's activities for what they were. That was not because Boyd was especially good at what she did; on the contrary, Union soldiers frequently intercepted her messages. Instead, Boyd benefited from the sexist assumption that women were incapable of being spies. Many military officials believed that women were not intelligent enough to remember detailed military informa-

tion. Nor would a true Southern lady stoop to such a devious activity as espionage. Despite the evidence, Union leaders did not wish to believe that such an innocent-seeming young woman could be a spy.

As a result, Boyd not only continued but expanded her activities. In 1862, for instance, Federal troops withdrawing from Front Royal, Virginia, planned to burn several local bridges to block a Confederate army advance. Boyd somehow learned of the scheme and set out to warn the Confederates. To reach the right people, though, she needed Federal permission to pass through the city. "Knowing Colonel Fillebrowne [a Union officer] was never displeased by a little flattery and a few delicate attentions," she recalled later, "I went to the florist and chose a very handsome bouquet, which I sent to him with my compliments and a request that he would be so kind as to permit me to return to Front Royal."[81] The stratagem worked. Boyd successfully passed on the information, and the Confederate troops recaptured the town.

Methods and Activities

Other spies may have been less beautiful, but they had other ways of gleaning important information. Rose Greenhow, for example, was a well-respected member of Washington society. Although a known

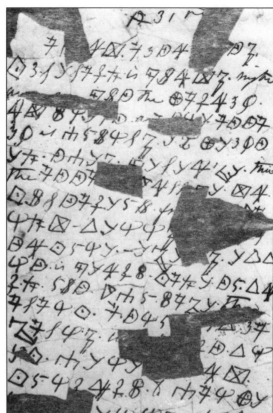

Confederate sympathizer Rose Greenhow is pictured with her daughter (left). A Southern spy, Greenhow sent coded messages (right) to the Confederate army from her home in Washington, D.C.

Confederate sympathizer, she was privy to political discussions with prominent Union military and government leaders. Then she transmitted useful information to General P.G.T. Beauregard via secret codes. Some of these codes were simple substitution ciphers in which one letter stood for another, but Greenhow also passed on sensitive information by raising and lowering the window shades around her Washington home. "But for you there would have been no battle of Bull Run,"[82]

Confederate president Jefferson Davis told her in recognition of her contribution to that early Confederate victory.

The Union had spies as well. Pauline Cushman, a professional actress who was born in New Orleans, put her theatrical talents to good use during the war. She caused quite a stir one night in a Northern theater when she interrupted a performance with an impromptu and apparently serious "Here's to Jeff Davis and the Southern Confederacy!"[83] It was all a ruse, however, designed to lull the South into thinking that she was on their side. Cushman headed south, where she used the guise of a pro-Confederate woman to spy for the Union; in this role she compiled lists of ardent Confederacy supporters, learned about enemy fortifications, and traveled frequently with messages for Union officials.

A few spies set up complex networks for gathering and disseminating what they learned. Richmond native Elizabeth Van Lew, for instance, organized a spy ring dedicated to passing on information to Union officers. Her sources included Confederate officials and wealthy members of Richmond society who often gathered at her home; they also included Union soldiers who were being held in Richmond's Libby Prison. To send her messages, Van Lew used a secret cipher, the key to which she carried in her watch, and an elaborate series of carriers, many of them slaves. She could be devious indeed, as the following description of her activities suggests:

Every day two of her trusty negro servants drove into [downtown]

Elizabeth Van Lew entertained Confederate officers at this elegant Richmond home in order to gather information for the Union army.

Women of the Civil War

Richmond with something to sell. . . . These negroes wore great, strong brogans [shoes], with soles of immense thickness. . . . Shoes were pretty scarce in the Confederacy in those days, but Miss Van Lew's servants had two pairs each and changed them every day. They never wore out of Richmond in the afternoon the same shoes they wore into the city in the morning. The soles of these shoes were double and hollow, and in them were carried through the lines letters, maps, plans, etc., which were regularly delivered to General [Ulysses] Grant at City Point the next morning.[84]

Like Greenhow, Van Lew used her society connections to gather information and to evade detection; it seemed inconceivable to many people that an upper-class woman would indulge in spy work. But Van Lew had another way of escaping suspicion. She pretended to be eccentric, even perhaps a little insane. Known as "Crazy Bet," she dressed oddly and wandered through the streets singing and chanting nonsensically to herself. It was all an act designed to make people think that she was mentally incapable of carrying out anti-Confederacy activities.

Suspicion and Arrest

Still, few female spies avoided suspicion entirely. While some Richmond residents were fooled by Van Lew's actions, others were not. One angry citizen wrote a letter to a newspaper in which he complained about her attentions to the Union prisoners and charged that she was not-so-secretly giving aid to the enemy. Despite Rose Greenhow's high-placed friends in the Union government, she eventually caught the eye of Northern intelligence officials. Even Boyd was captured by Union officers and charged with spying.

Here again, though, gender brought leniency. Soldiers commonly treated women, particular those of the upper classes, with the respect and courtesy of a chivalrous age. The first time she was caught passing on sensitive information, Belle Boyd was reprimanded and released, though a male spy in the same position might well have been put to death. Indeed, no woman was put to death during the war for espionage. Pauline Cushman was sentenced to die after being arrested by Confederate generals John Hunt Morgan and Nathan Bedford Forrest; but she was freed by advancing Union troops before the sentence could be carried out, and many historians doubt that Morgan and Forrest actually intended to execute her in any case.

Even when women spent time in jail for their spying activities, their sentences were usually not severe. Boyd's penalty for the incident at Front Royal was just two months in jail, and according to one historian she was "well fed and comfortably housed"[85] during that time. After five months in a Washington prison, Rose Greenhow was released to the custody of the Confederacy. A Union spy named Mary Caroline Allan pleaded ill health, ended up in a hospital rather than in prison, and was eventually released on bail. Gender, it seems, nullified the enormity of their crimes.

Yet the female spies did not take up their work on the expectation that they would somehow evade capture and punishment. The spies were motivated, instead, by a deep-seated patriotism and a desire to do whatever they could to help their side. Their activities required tremendous courage—and also tremendous foolhardiness. Boyd, said a reporter of the time, was "insanely devoted to the rebel cause."[86]

Scouts, Couriers, and Saboteurs

Also more or less independent agents were the women who filled the roles of scouts, couriers, and saboteurs. Scouts guided soldiers through unfamiliar territory; they also went out, usually at night, to observe enemy troops and fortifications. While most scouts were men, some were women. Fifteen-year-old Emma Sansom, a staunch Confederate from Alabama, led a group of Southern cavalrymen across a shallow spot in a local river after Union troops had burned the only bridge. Thirty years later, a Southern writer memorialized her heroism in a poem, and a statue of her was raised in a nearby town.

Other women served as couriers, or messengers. Military commanders sometimes preferred to have women carry important information to headquarters or to other generals. Not only did using a woman free up men for fighting, but women were less likely to be searched if they were captured, especially if they were native to the region. Anna Campbell, a Union sympathizer in Alabama, once traveled seventy miles in a marathon day-and-a-half horseback ride in order to bring a vital message to a general. On the Confederate side, Molly Tynes of Virginia made an 1863 midnight ride to warn the citizens of Wytheville of an approaching attack by Federal troops.

A few women served as saboteurs during the war. These women were usually enthusiastic Confederates in border states or in areas occupied by Federal troops, though sometimes they were Union supporters who lived in the Confederacy. While few seem to have engaged in physical violence, they nevertheless damaged army wagons, burned supply centers, and destroyed roads and bridges. Sarah Jane Smith, a Missouri Confederate, got her start in sabotage at the age of fourteen. Among her exploits was the slicing of several miles of Union telegraph cables—a matter so serious

Frank Thompson

One of the more unusual stories of the Civil War concerns Sarah Emma Edmonds. Born in Canada in 1841, Edmonds ran away from home as a teenager in order to escape from her abusive father. She disguised herself as a man, presumably because she could more easily earn a living that way, and sold bibles for a time. Not long before the war broke out, she moved to Michigan. In the spring of 1861, Edmonds enlisted in a local volunteer regiment under the name Franklin Thompson.

As Frank, Edmonds was a popular member of the regiment. Most of her companions never caught on to her actual gender, though at least one knew. "My friend Frank is a female," wrote Jerome Robbins in his diary, as quoted in *Notable American Women*, edited by Edward T. James. Robbins did not seem particularly astonished at the news, nor does he appear to have shared the secret with anyone else. Although there is little evidence that Edmonds ever actually fought in battle, she was certainly used as a mail clerk and a (supposedly male) nurse, and she may have served as a spy as well.

In April 1863, Edmonds deserted from her regiment, moved to Ohio, and gave up playing the part of a man for good. She wrote a book, *Nurse and Spy in the Union Army*, which was published in 1865 under her own name. In the book, Edmonds described some of her wartime experiences. However, she suggested that she had served as a woman; she gave no indication that she had actually played the role of a male soldier. The book was a popular seller at the time.

The story of Sarah Emma Edmonds might have ended there, but in 1884 Edmonds (by then the wife of Linus Seelye) applied for a pension given only to army veterans. Many of her former army companions attested to her good character and to her military service, although most had not known previously that she was a woman. That July, Congress awarded her the pension she sought. She collected twelve dollars every month thereafter until her death in 1898.

that Federal officials sentenced her to death when she was captured, though they later commuted the sentence to imprisonment for the rest of the war.

All-Woman Militias

In several parts of the country, women took on certain traditionally male duties simply because the men were not there to fill them. Women sometimes served as members of informal militias, organized to defend their communities in case of enemy attack. Most local militias were never called on to fight off invasions. Nor did most of them last throughout the war. One that did both, however, was the women's militia of LaGrange, Georgia.

The LaGrange militia was the brain-child of Nancy Morgan, a young woman of the town. In a conversation with her friend Mary Heard, Morgan pointed out that LaGrange was completely defenseless against Yankee marauders and escaped prisoners. Nearly all the men were at the front, after all, and none of the women of the town knew how to shoot a gun. Appalled by the thought of a Yankee invasion, Heard asked what they could do to remedy the situation. As Morgan described the scene years later, the following dialogue then ensued:

[Morgan said,] "We might form a military company of women."

"Did you ever hear of a military company of women?" said [Heard].

"No, but that doesn't matter," said I.

"No, I suppose not," said she.

"I've got my grandfather's old flint-lock fowling-piece," said I.

"I've got an old rifle," said she.

"We'll issue a call," said I, "and we'll organize a company. At least we can defend our homes, and if they want us at the front—well, we'll be ready."[87]

The company soon was formed, with Morgan as commander. Known as the "Nancy Harts" after a Revolutionary War heroine from Georgia, the group consisted of forty or more of the town's young women. Twice a week the Nancy Harts practiced target shooting in a nearby field. This was a difficult business; not only did the women have little experience with firearms, but their weapons were old, rusty, and prone to misfiring. One woman accidentally hit a hornet's nest on an early attempt. But before long, one member reported with pride, the women of the company had gotten used to firing their weapons and had become expert shots.

The Nancy Harts also drilled on a regular basis. They had no uniforms as such, since buttons and fabric were needed for the soldiers at the front. Still, they donned "feminine dress of ruffled skirts and flowered or feathered hats," as one participant recalled, and marched through the streets of the town "ready and anxious for combat or to be called to field duty."[88]

Their chance did arrive, but very late in the war. In early 1865 a group of Union soldiers approached the community. They were met by the Nancy Harts, who stood blocking the road with their guns on their shoulders. More touched and amused than irritated by the sight of the women clutching their antique firearms, their commander accepted an invitation to tea at one woman's house, instructed his troops to treat the other members of the company with kindness and respect, and passed by without inflicting major damage on the town. "They [the Federal troops] came, they saw, but *we* conquered," one member of the organization wrote with pride years later. "The engagement was brief but decisive."[89]

Albert Cashier and Jennie Hodgers

The Nancy Harts may never have fired a shot at an actual enemy, but some women did exactly that. In August 1862, the men

Sally Bull, second corporal in the Nancy Harts.

of northwestern Illinois banded together to form a new regiment. Among the early enlisters was a local farmer named Albert Cashier. Though small, quiet, and somewhat unfriendly, Cashier was a good and dedicated soldier. His commanding officer believed him to be healthy, dependable, and brave, and he chose Cashier for scout patrol. On one occasion, Cashier knocked down a Confederate sentry, stole the rebel's gun, and retreated to safety.

After serving a three-year term, Cashier returned to Illinois, where he lived for the rest of his long life. "He was well liked," reported a historian in one of the towns where he lived. "[He] kept himself clean and neat, marched in patriotic parades in complete Civil War uniform . . . and was considered an asset to the community."[90] Then, in 1911, almost a half century after his enlistment, Cashier was hit by a car and broke his leg. A doctor was called and examined the patient—and made a startling discovery. Albert Cashier was not a man at all. "He" was actually a woman—an Irish immigrant whose real name was Jennie Hodgers.

Female soldiers were not unheard of before the Civil War. Deborah Sampson of Massachusetts, for example, fought under an assumed name during the Revolutionary War. Nor did nineteenth-century Americans dismiss the possibility that women soldiers might be in the ranks. Indeed, rumors of such troops ran rampant. "A Pennsylvania girl who has been living as a soldier in the southwest for ten months," read a typical news account of the time, "says she has discovered a great many females among the soldiers."[91] Like other such reports, though, this one included no names, regiments, or other identifying details, and could not be verified.

The Officers of the Nancy Harts

No complete roster of the Nancy Harts exists, but a list of the group's officers and a few miscellaneous members has been preserved. Each woman had a suitably military title. The officers included:

Nancy Morgan, Captain

Mary Heard, First Lieutenant

Alice Smith, Second Lieutenant

Andelia Bull, Third Lieutenant

Augusta Hill, First Sergeant

Pack Beall, Second Sergeant

Leila Pullen, First Corporal

Sally Bull, Second Corporal

Caroline Ware Poythress, Third Corporal

There were many connections between the women. All the officers were members of the First Methodist Church of LaGrange, Georgia, and many had attended school together. Andelia and Sally Bull were sisters; so were Nancy Morgan and Augusta Hill. Several of the officers had sisters or other relatives within the ranks. The Nancy Harts were a close-knit group.

In fact, a great deal remains unknown about the women who dressed as men and served in the Civil War armies. Even the number of female troops during the conflict is open to a great deal of question. Historians have compiled lists of soldiers known to be women, but most agree that there were many more than the names appearing on the lists indicate. The best estimates today suggest that between five hundred and one thousand women took up arms and joined one army or the other.

The number of women soldiers remains unknown mainly because their very existence was a secret. Since women were forbidden to enter the Union and Confederate armies, all who enlisted did so without leaving official records of their true identity. As the case of Jennie Hodgers shows, some women soldiers may well have carried their secrets to the grave. Indeed, digging in and around Civil War battlefields has revealed a handful of women buried in uniform. In 1934, for instance, a Tennessee man found human remains while planting a flower bed at his home near the Shiloh battleground. Subsequent investigation revealed that the site was the burial ground for nine Civil War soldiers: eight men and one woman.

Many reports of female soldiers, however, like that of the Pennsylvania girl mentioned above, are vague and unverifiable. Similarly, some women who claimed later to have been active in the war may have exaggerated or invented their accomplishments. In a book written two years after the end of the war, a Louisiana woman named Loreta Velasquez said she served undetected as Confederate soldier Harry T. Buford, but could not prove her claim. Several women made similar assertions, with the same uncertain result.

Keeping Secrets

For a woman to maintain a male disguise for weeks, months, or even years was extremely hard, but by no means impossible. Several women, like Jennie Hodgers, already had experience passing themselves off as men outside the military. Sarah Rosetta Wakeman, for example, had disguised herself earlier as a man so she could work on a New York State canal. From there it was a simple matter to join the army as Private Lyons Wakeman. "I saw some soldiers," she explained in a terse letter home to her family. "They wanted I should enlist and so I did."[92] Her disguise was obviously compelling.

In fact, several factors made it possible for a determined woman to enlist. Recruiters could not demand proof of identity; there were no driver's licenses or social security cards during the time. Nor did most soldiers receive a thorough

Sarah Edmonds posed as a man to join the Union army. She is pictured (left) as Private Franklin Thompson, her male persona, and (right) as herself.

medical exam before enlisting. The medical exam given to Sarah Emma Edmonds, who enlisted as Private Franklin Thompson, consisted of "a firm handshake"[93] and nothing more. Even in camp and on the battlefield, it was possible for a woman to evade detection. Levels of personal hygiene were not what they are today, and soldiers seldom removed their clothing to wash or sleep.

Even physical appearance was not necessarily a problem. Because of poor nutrition and frequent disease, many adult males of the time were noticeably scrawny. Both armies included teenage boys whose voices had not yet changed and who had no facial hair. At the time of the Civil War, too, women invariably wore skirts and kept their hair long. A figure with short hair, pants, and a soldier's cap was automatically assumed to be male. "No one thought of finding a woman in a soldier's dress,"[94] one man wrote, explaining why he never guessed that one of his comrades was female.

Being a woman soldier, however, was far from easy. Most of the women who served worried that their secret would be revealed. A wound or a serious illness could send a soldier to the hospital, where her sex would probably be discovered. One woman's secret was discovered when she fainted and her fellow soldiers started to give her a warm bath. Most women chose to remain somewhat aloof from their companions, not wanting anyone to get to know them too well. The women soldiers likewise worked hard to disguise telltale feminine speech, looks, and mannerisms.

Despite all their efforts, though, some women could not sustain the charade for long. Two new recruits were found out when they tried to catch apples thrown to them in their nonexistent aprons. Mary Smith was discovered while washing dishes at an encampment: "[She gave an] unmistakable twist to the dishcloth in wringing it out," explained an observer, "that no [man] could ever successfully counterfeit."[95] And several women found proof of their sex absolutely impossible to disguise. "The other night the Corporal had a baby," reported a Union soldier with utter astonishment, "for the Cpl. turned out to be a woman!"[96]

The best way to pass as a man was to be a good soldier, and plenty of the women who served were exactly that.

Annie Lillybridge of Michigan was said to have shot a Confederate captain, and Minnesota's Frances Clayton was known by her companions as "a good fighting man."[97] Women who successfully concealed their sex did all the lifting, marching, and drilling that their male comrades did, usually without complaint. Their courage and their emotional strength further made them seem like men, for women of the time were believed incapable of such activity.

As a result, many of these women succeeded in fooling even their closest companions for a surprisingly long time. No one seems to have caught on to Rosetta Wakeman's true identity until her death. A New Jersey woman, Elizabeth Niles, apparently fought throughout the war without anyone noticing that she was female. Upon hearing that Albert Cashier had actually been a woman, at least one member of Cashier's regiment was thoroughly shocked. "There was never a doubt about that fellow,"[98] he said, pointing out that he had harbored accurate suspicions about the sex of several other recruits. Presumably, some women carried out the charade with such confidence and skill that their sex was never identified.

Patriotism, Profit, and Love

The women who served as soldiers had varied reasons for being there. For some, the attraction was patriotism and adventure, along with the opportunity to take on dress, manners, and activities ordinarily forbidden them by society. Certainly Jennie Hodgers and Rosetta Wakeman, both of whom dressed as men beyond the battlefield, fell into this category. So did the Confederacy's Loreta Velasquez, if her story can be taken as at least partly true: "I was perfectly wild on the subject of war,"[99] she wrote in her account of wartime service. Another woman who joined for the adventure was the Union's Elizabeth Compton, who had a much harder time concealing her sex, but who enlisted in a new regiment each time she was found out.

Other women were motivated largely by money. Soldiers were not paid especially well, but their salaries were much higher than those of nurses or laundresses. Indeed, soldiers earned more money than almost any occupation open to women at the time. In addition to wanting to experience adventure and see the world from a masculine perspective, Rosetta Wakeman was also eager to increase her earnings. "I knew that I could help you more to leave home than to stay there with you,"[100] she wrote to her family, and her letters reveal that she sent most of her pay home to support her parents.

More women, though, enlisted for love. Some women refused to let their

A Letter Home

Sarah Rosetta Wakeman, who served in the Union army as Private Lyons Wakeman, wrote letters home to her parents in upstate New York. Early in the conflict she signed her letters "Rosetta," evidently unafraid that her true identity would be revealed; later, she took to calling herself "Edwin" in her signatures. The following is an excerpt from one of Wakeman's typical letters home, as quoted in *An Uncommon Soldier*, edited by Lauren Cook Burgess:

I don't know how long before I shall have to go into the field of battle, [but] for my part I don't care. I don't feel afraid to go. I don't believe there are any Rebel's bullet[s] made for me yet. Nor I don't care if there is. I am as independent as a hog on the ice. If it is God['s] will for me to fall in the field of battle, it is my will to go and never return home.

men go to war without them, and for various reasons they were unwilling to follow these loved ones as camp women. Frances Day, also known as Frank Mayne, enlisted in a Pennsylvania regiment along with her husband. Annie Lillybridge and Frances Clayton also followed their lovers into battle. Amy Clarke, a Confederate who served under the name of Richard Anderson, joined a Louisiana cavalry unit with her husband; according to some sources, she also served in a Tennessee regiment after his death.

"It Is What I Have Wished For"

The grave marker of the Union spy Elizabeth Van Lew reads, "She risked everything that is dear to man—friends, fortune, comfort, life itself."[101] The women who served their armies as spies, soldiers, scouts, and sentries all chose occupations which involved both danger and secrecy. Moreover, the women who carried out these jobs were going far beyond the normal behavior expected of women at the time. It would have been easy—and quite understandable—for these women to have taken a different path.

Indeed, almost any other wartime service would have been less difficult than the active duties these women chose. Pamphleteers, after all, contributed to the war effort as much as spies and saboteurs, and did so under their own names and from a position of relative safety. Battlefield nurses did not need to disguise their gender, but still came nearly as close to the action as did the female soldiers. And a woman did not need to wear a uniform in order to follow her husband into the army; she could have become a cook or a laundress instead.

But the women who took on the roles described in this chapter did in fact reject these other possibilities. Instead, they opted for danger and secrecy. Despite the risks and the hardships—or perhaps because of them—it is clear that these women genuinely liked what they did. Serving as a soldier, a scout, or a spy brought them a sense of purpose they could not get from nursing, managing a family farm, or becoming involved in political questions. "I feel perfectly happy," wrote Rosetta Wakeman in 1863. "If I go into a battle I shall be alright. It is what I have wish[ed] for a good while."[102]

Chapter 6:
African American Women

☙

African American women experienced the Civil War in a variety of ways. Northern or Southern, free or slave, black women had to deal with everything their white counterparts dealt with—and more. Practically any role filled by a white woman during the war was filled, at some point along the way, by an African American woman, too. But because of racial prejudice, poverty, and lack of education, the roles were generally much more difficult for black women.

Many slave women bravely and creatively escaped from their owners when Union troops came near. Some Northern black women boldly spoke up about the need to end slavery altogether, often before the region as a whole was ready to hear what they had to say. And black nurses, washerwomen, and cooks served despite obstacles that white camp women never had to overcome. African American women were hardly content to wait for the Civil War to bring freedom and opportunity to them. Instead, they used the war to help get what they wanted themselves.

Black Women of the North

Black women represented only a small proportion of the population of the North. In addition to more than 400,000 slaves in the loyal but slaveholding border states, the North as a whole had perhaps 350,000 free blacks, about half of them female. Still, the role of black women in the war went far beyond their numbers. While Abraham Lincoln was—at least at first—careful not to frame the conflict as a battle against slavery, most free African American women in the North knew perfectly well that victory might mean the end of the institution. Moreover, they knew that by offering their full support to the government and the soldiers, they might show dubious whites that they were intelligent, loyal, and resourceful. For both these reasons, black Northern women were involved in many aspects of the war effort.

Many of these efforts paralleled those of Northern white women. Soldiers' aid societies, for instance, sprang up in the black communities of Philadelphia and other cities, just as they did in white neighborhoods and towns. The typical African American woman was poor in comparison to the whites of the North, so aid was relatively limited. Still, every penny, blanket, and item of clothing collected made a difference to the soldiers, white or black, who eventually received it.

Many Northern black women went into nursing, too, or followed the Union troops as washerwomen or cooks. Because of racial prejudice, these women were paid less than their white counterparts. Prejudice also made them the target of scorn among whites, both male and female; it was common for black women to be criticized for a perceived lack of commitment to their jobs. "[My] hardest work," wrote a white nurse, "was to keep two colored ladies . . . steady to the work

An unidentified black woman (at far right) is the cook for the Union troops posed in front of their tents.

of scrubbing the lower deck"[103] of the hospital ship where they were stationed.

Nevertheless, most of the black cooks, nurses, and laundresses worked extremely hard. The contributions of these women were invaluable. Susie Baker joined the Thirty-third U.S. Colored Troops as a washerwoman, but soon moved into nursing and cooking as well. She also learned the rudiments of cleaning and firing muskets and tutored the troops in reading and writing, skills which she had secretly learned as a young slave. "My hands have never left undone anything they could do toward aid and comfort"[104] of the army, she wrote many years later.

Spies and Abolitionists

A few black women took on more dramatic roles in the conflict. Among the spies of the Civil War, for instance, was a young freed slave named Mary Elizabeth Bowser. Bowser had belonged to the family of Union spymaster Elizabeth Van Lew. Through family connections, Van Lew found Bowser a position as a domestic servant in the home of Confederate president Jefferson Davis. Once in Davis's house, Bowser passed important military information to Van Lew and her associates on the outside. Well over a century afterward, Bowser's bravery won her a spot in the U.S. Army's Intelligence Hall of Fame.

Other African American women took up the cause of abolition. The black women who were active in this movement were relatively small in numbers, but they were enthusiastic in spirit and thoroughly committed to their cause. Most black women abolitionists had been born free, mostly in the North, but some were freed and escaped slaves. Indeed, several of the best-known women of the Civil War were abolitionists who had once been slaves.

Foremost among these women was Sojourner Truth. Born about 1797, Truth had spent her first thirty years as a slave in New York State. Later, she had come to the public's attention as a plain-spoken advocate for the rights of blacks and women. She had remarkable personal charisma, and even her enemies admitted that she was an excellent debater. While the war was being fought, Truth crisscrossed her adopted home state of Michigan, drumming up support for the Northern army and speaking to everyone she could about the evils of slavery. In late 1864 she spoke with Abraham Lincoln at the White House, and soon after that she was appointed to a position working with newly freed slaves.

Staunch abolitionist Harriet Tubman, more than twenty years younger than Truth, had escaped from a Maryland plantation in 1849 and safely made her

Sojourner Truth described her life as a slave and an abolitionist in her autobiography, Narrative of Sojourner Truth, a Northern Slave.

way to Philadelphia. Over the next dozen years, she made nineteen courageous trips back into slave territory to lead others to freedom as a "conductor" on the network of escape known as the Underground Railroad. The risk was great, but Tubman had extraordinary determination. Estimates of the number of slaves she rescued range as high as three hundred.

When the Civil War broke out, Tubman volunteered her services. She traveled to Beaufort, South Carolina, near the center of a coastal region that had been reclaimed by Union troops. Thoroughly committed to the cause of abolition, Tubman served the army as nurse, spy, scout, and more. Her experiences evading detection in Maryland helped her travel secretly within the surrounding Confederate territory, watching for military postings and troop movements. And her reputation as a committed abolitionist encouraged the local blacks to trust her with sensitive information. The Union army benefited tremendously from her work.

Other female black abolitionists helped the Union cause. A free black author named Frances Watkins Harper lectured on the topic of slavery throughout the Midwest; much of her writing income went to help the newly freed slaves. Another free woman, a teacher named Mary Ann Shadd Cary, helped Midwestern governors recruit black men to act as soldiers. And another woman, Sarah Remond, traveled to England and encouraged support for the Union cause. But these women were merely the most visible. As one historian has pointed out, "For each Negro woman whose work was recognized, hundreds were quietly working behind the scenes."[105]

Slave Women

But at the beginning of the Civil War, most African American women could do very little for the Union cause. The reason was simple: They were enslaved.

The 4 million or so Southern slaves, half of them female, significantly outnumbered the free blacks who lived around the country. Even Boston, a big city with strong antislavery leanings, was home to only a few thousand African Americans at the eve of the war. In 1861, by far the greatest number of black women in the United States were Southern slaves.

Slavery at the Start of the War

The daily life of a Southern slave woman at the start of the Civil War varied considerably, depending on her duties, her location, and the character of her owners. Some slave women labored in the fields, planting and harvesting cotton, rice, and sugar. They worked from before dawn to after dusk, in the winter cold and in the summer sun. Others served as cooks, washerwomen, or personal servants for women and girls of the master's household. The house slaves were generally considered to have the better jobs, but even their lives were by no means easy.

Another difference in the experience of slave women involved surroundings. Most slaves lived and worked with many others in their condition. In contrast, other slave women lived on small and rather isolated farms where they might be one of only a handful of black people. Both situations had advantages and disadvantages. The work on the larger farms tended to be more difficult and less varied; but the slave women on the smaller farms did not have the companionship that the larger farms could offer.

Finally, a woman's experience of slavery was tightly connected to the character of her owners. The class of Southern slaveholders included all-too-many men and women who treated their slaves with contempt. They spoke to them rudely and angrily; they stinted on feeding, clothing, and sheltering their slaves; they humiliated their slaves and forced them to work at an inhuman pace. Their use of physical punishment, too, common among most slaveowners, often bordered on the sadistic.

Of course, not all slaveholders were so cruel. Some slave women had masters and mistresses who treated them with relative kindness. These owners made sure that their slaves had enough to eat and did their best not to overwork them. Many whipped slaves only for serious disciplinary breaches; a few never beat their slaves. Regardless of her individual experience, however, a slave longed for freedom and a better life. By 1862, when the Emancipation Proclamation was announced, she began to believe the war could achieve that goal.

Southern slave women, however, were hardly passive observers of the war effort. In various ways they did what they could to help the Union—and to help themselves. As the war dragged on, most slave women took every opportunity they could to be disobedient, to interfere with the Confederate war effort, and to take advantage of the chaos created by the war. Slowly in some cases and much more rapidly in others, they were working for their own freedom.

Within a few weeks of the April 1861 firing on Fort Sumter, most Southern slave women were aware that war was underway. The news traveled mainly through word of mouth, since nearly all slave women were illiterate. Information about the war came from two main sources. It was usually most reliable when it came from overheard conversations among literate whites, many of whom openly discussed matters of politics even when their slaves were present. "People talk before them [the slaves] as if they were chairs and tables,"[106] wrote diarist Mary Chesnut, who was nevertheless powerless to stop her influential friends from holding forth in the presence of serving girls and butlers. The typical slave who overheard gave no sign of understanding, but passed on the news as soon as she could.

Much less reliable was the news that came directly from the slavemasters themselves. Many slaveholders talked with their slaves, both formally and informally, about the war. For the most part, they tried to encourage the African Americans to see the Confederacy as fighting a noble battle against evildoers from the North. Some slaveholders did their job extremely well. "Us all thought de Yankees was some kin' of debils an' we was skeered to death of 'em,"[107] explained Mollie Williams, who had heard her master demonize Northerners on many occasions during the early part of the war.

But for those who had alternate sources of information, it soon became clear that the masters were not telling the full truth. Slave women quickly grasped the reality of the war: It was a conflict between their masters, who approved of and supported the institution of slavery, and the Yankees, who opposed it. As these women saw it, the war could mean an end to their enslavement. "I started prayin' for freedom," recalled Mississippi slave Dora Franks, "and all de rest of de women did de same thing."[108]

At first, though, the war had little direct effect on the average slave woman. The initial fighting was concentrated in a handful of seaports and a few areas of the upper South. Apart from those who lived near these battlegrounds, daily life for most women slaves continued much as it had before. The front lines of the

Many black women realized that the war could mean an end to their enslavement, dramatized in this drawing of an overseer brandishing a whip at a woman shackled at the hands.

Union army were too far away to have much impact on the slave women of the middle and lower South.

Wartime Effects on a Slave's Duties

Still, the war brought slave women a few important changes. Some slave women found that the war afforded them a sort of vacation. The Confederacy had a great need for soldiers, and during the early stages of the war many Southern men were eager to enlist. The list of new Confederate soldiers included not only slaveowners, but also their sons, their brothers, and their hired overseers. One effect of all these enlistments was to leave the slaves in the hands of many white women and not very many white men.

The lack of white men emboldened some of the slave women—and men, too—to slacken the pace of their work. In one notable case, a whole group of Mississippi slaves went on a virtual month-long strike in 1863. There was little to stop them. The South did not have enough overseers to go around, and many of the white

Songs of Freedom

Slaves had a long and rich history of singing as they worked. Most masters seldom thought about the custom; to the extent that they did, they approved of it, believing that the singing indicated the slaves were happy and content. However, many slave songs had double meanings. In coded language, they expressed the slaves' desire to be free, and sometimes even indicated plans for escape. Often the songs contained biblical imagery of persecution and the promised land. "Go Down, Moses," for example, could notify Maryland slaves that Harriet Tubman—known as "Moses" among African Americans—was nearby. "I Am Bound for the Land of Canaan" spoke not simply of the afterlife but also of the prosperity and freedom available in the North. And the song "Follow the Drinking Gourd," popular in parts of the western Confederacy, gave hidden directions to runaway slaves traveling north toward the Ohio River.

As the war dragged on and more and more slaves escaped to Union lines, the images of freedom in African Americans' songs grew less guarded. "Go Down, Abraham," sang a woman in a Washington contraband camp, as quoted in Stephen Currie, *Music in the Civil War:*

Away down in Dixie's land;

Tell Jeff Davis

To let my people go.

Another popular camp song was called "I Thank God That I Am Free at Last." And another was "Oh, Freedom," still popular today, which includes the lines:

And before I'd be a slave

I'd be buried in my grave

And go home to my Lord and be free.

Just as music had expressed African Americans' concerns and hopes when they were enslaved, so were these songs used to do the same once they were free.

mistresses proved less than adept at managing their plantations. A few more or less gave up. "We cannot exert any authority," wrote an exhausted white woman in 1863. "I beg our [slaves] to do what little is done."[109]

But in other places, the pace of the slave women's work often increased. Because the South lacked economic self-sufficiency, Confederate leaders urged farms, plantations, and industries to produce all that they could. The burden of this task fell upon the slaves, who were exhorted to work harder and harder—often at or indeed past their capacity to do so. Breaks became fewer and shorter, and beatings for not meeting quotas became more common.

Slave women were more seriously affected by the increased workload than were slave men. Many of the white men who went off to war took male slaves with them as personal servants. Later, some slave men were taken from their homes and put to work building bridges and digging tunnels for the army. These slaves were by necessity strong and relatively young; their absence forced the others, notably the women, to take up the slack. "[I] plowed [with] a mule and a wild 'un at that," complained a young woman who ordinarily would have been assigned to less stressful work. "Sometimes me hand get so cold I jes' cry."[110]

A final issue for African American women in the early days of the war involved the breakup of slave families. Many of the separations involved those slave men forced into service for the Confederate army while their women stayed at home. Being separated from their men was no easier for the slave women than it was for the Southern white women whose husbands were at the front. Indeed, it was more difficult for the slaves, because they had been given no choice in the matter.

A more serious and more permanent type of separation involved separation through sale. No law gave slave couples the right to stay together or to be sold as a pair. Neither, for that matter, did slave children have any legal right to stay with their parents. Some slaveowners, knowing they would soon be going to war, hurried to sell off as many slaves as they could before they left. Quite often the sales meant breaking up families forever. "She am so old 'n feeble," mourned one woman about her grandmother, who was separated from her during the war. "I hates dat, but don't say nothin' at all."[111]

The Coming of the Yankees

For most slave women, the biggest changes took place when the Union front lines came closer to the farms. As the

Some plantation owners sold off their slaves before going to war. It was not uncommon for members of slave families to be separated and sold to different buyers.

Yankees approached, excitement usually grew on the plantations where the slaves worked. The slave women were careful to avoid showing their true feelings to the masters and overseers. Nevertheless, they were well aware of what was going on. In particular, they knew that military success on the part of the Union could translate to freedom for the slaves.

In some cases, slave women decided to hurry freedom along. These women were not content to wait for Northern troops to set them free; instead, they chose to do the work themselves. Under cover of darkness, they left their homes and headed toward the Union lines. One group of South Carolina slave women traveled eighty miles to a Union encampment, carrying their babies as best they could. "[I] tinks ole missis wait good," laughed one of these women, imagining the shock of her owner upon discovering that the slaves had vanished. "She call Delia loud den me but she never get none [of us to] breakfast dat day!"[112]

More often, though, slave women waited on their plantations until the Yankees actually arrived, in part to avoid the risks of transporting children. Traveling at night with small children slowed down and tired out a fleeing slave. The possibility that a child might cry was also a danger; a squalling baby could easily give away an escape attempt. The rigors of the trail could also be hard on young children who were too large to be carried. Because of the need to protect their children, slave women were less likely than slave men to make a run for the nearest Union line.

It was also true that slave women were often more closely watched than slave men were. While circumstances varied considerably, slave women tended to be assigned tasks close to the plantation house. Similarly, while slave men sometimes were sent on errands that would take them off the plantation, slave women usually were not. Moreover, once a few slaves—generally men—had run away from a plantation, the slaveholder typically cracked down on the rest. Eliza Ann Mathey's husband, for example, escaped from the couple's Mississippi owners; but when she tried to follow, she found that security was much too tight.

Hostility, Theft, and Violence

That was not to say that the women who stayed continued to submit easily to slavery. On the contrary, as the Union troops approached, slave women became increasingly hostile toward their white

---

"Everybody Cried"

The ranks of slave women included some who chose to stand by their owners as long as possible, though exactly how many slave women remained loyal to their masters and mistresses is unknown. Diaries and reminiscences of white Southerners often refer to their sorrow as the so-called betrayal of slaves who ran off as soon as they could. Still, those records make frequent references to slaves—slave women, in particular—who refused to leave, even when doing so would have been very easy.

Whites, however, are not the only source of this information. Some African Americans, then and afterwards, spoke of the strong positive feelings they felt for their owners. "If all slaves had belonged to white folks like ours, there wouldn't have been any freedom wanted," said Harriet McFarlin Payne many years after the end of slavery, as quoted in B.A. Botkin, *Lay My Burden Down*. "We had the best mistress and master in the world," remembered Millie Evans. "Everybody cried when the Yankees cried out: 'Free.'"

For other loyal slave women, their reluctance to leave may have been fear of the Yankees, anxiety about the unknown, or a perhaps misplaced sense of responsibility. Whatever the cause, some slave women did stay with their masters' families—and a few, such as Payne and Evans, expressed real regrets about the end of the institution.

masters. Again, this hostility was rarely out in the open; rudeness or flagrant disobedience could still earn a woman a beating. But in many small ways, slave women began to refuse to allow their owners to control them.

Subtle disobedience took many forms. A slave could, for example, hear and agree to instructions from a mistress and then simply fail to follow them. Many women who served as house slaves were told to help conceal the family treasures as the Yankees neared. That meant driving cows into the backwoods, pushing bags of flour and meal into cracks in the basement, and burying silverware in the garden. Some slave women, loyal to the last, refused to tell Yankee invaders where the goods were hidden. But many others were only too ready to tell the location of the valuables. "Our old cook," lamented one white woman, "who had been the most indulged and well treated servant imaginable . . . betrayed their hiding place."[113]

As Union armies neared, women slaves turned to petty theft of household objects, sometimes for possible use after emancipation, other times to irritate and annoy the slaveholders. A Mississippi slave mistress, missing some valuable objects one day, discovered that her favored slave Hannah was concealing a butter dish, a silver goblet, and several dresses inside her mattress. Hannah, it developed, was not the only slave who had run off with things, and the mistress had to spend precious time and energy hunting down the rest.

In a few cases during the war, slave women turned violent. The plantation owners tended to fear slave men a good deal more than slave women, but in several incidents slave women beat or even killed their owners. A white Alabama woman recorded the news in her diary of a "most atrocious murder"[114] in which a female slave who lived nearby had killed her mistress. In Georgia, another woman pushed her mistress into a fire. The victim only escaped when her assailant's clothes began to burn, and the slave was forced to let go in order to put out the flames.

The Contrabands

In many areas of the South, Yankee troops eventually did reach the plantations where slave women labored, awaiting freedom. The result was often a celebration. "[We] got together and laughed and sang and danced all night rejoicing,"[115] recalled Charity Jones about the reaction of the women on her plantation when the Northern soldiers arrived. For others, the delight may have been more muted, but the sentiments were usually the same.

To be sure, freedom was hardly easy for many of these women. While the war was still being fought, freedom depended on the presence of Federal troops, or on the ability of a slave woman to put plenty of distance between her and her former owners. Sometimes, when Northern soldiers moved on, masters would round up as many African Americans as they could and effectively enslave them again. Nor was the presence of the Yankees an unmixed blessing. Union soldiers sometimes raped the former slaves rather than offering them protection. Other Union troops raided the plantations and the countryside for food, sharply limiting what the African American women themselves could eat.

A further problem was that the Union was not always eager to take on escaped slaves. Very early in the war, in fact, the usual policy was to return runaways to their owners. That policy soon began to change as individual commanders in the Northern armies realized that keeping and freeing slaves struck a severe blow to the Confederacy. By the middle of 1862 virtually no Union generals returned fugitive slaves. Still, even then the runaways—usually known as "contrabands"—were not necessarily welcome in the Northern encampments. Many of the soldiers and officers were racist. Besides, the army had enough trou-

ble feeding, clothing, and moving its own troops, to say nothing of adding thousands of escaped slaves into the mix.

However, Federal leaders soon found ways to make use of the contrabands. The men were pressed into service as cooks, blacksmiths, and builders; later in the war they were permitted to serve as soldiers, too. The women presented a somewhat more complicated question. Former slave Elizabeth Kane followed her soldier husband, just as many white women did. "I washed for him during his entire service in the army," Kane recalled. "The officers let me live in a tent with my husband."[116] Several women, similarly, got jobs cooking for the soldiers.

A few women were taught to read and write in so-called freedmen's schools. Staffed mainly by Northern white abolitionist women, these schools gave the former slaves the basics of an education. Although some of the teachers were unprepared for the depths of their pupils' ignorance, the students were usually willing and eager to learn. "Altho' four months ago she could only read her alphabet," wrote one teacher of a woman named Susan, "now she can read understandingly . . . and is learning to write rapidly."[117]

But most freed women slaves were returned to plantations abandoned by

Freedmen's schools, staffed mainly by Northern white abolitionist women, gave former slaves and their children the basics of an education.

Southern slaveholders, hired to work for the Union. The idea was not necessarily a bad one. Unfortunately, its execution was. Conditions on the plantations were uncomfortably similar to those these women had recently escaped. The work was no easier, the pay was meager and sometimes nonexistent, and the promises of no physical punishment were not always observed. The camps in which these women lived were often squalid, too, although some did boast of churches and hospitals.

Still, the newly freed women who spent their time in the contraband camps were not beaten down by the reality of their situation. They had waited a lifetime for freedom, and now, at last, freedom was theirs. Some were offered paying jobs on the plantations belonging to their former owners; a few accepted, but many more did not. "No, Miss, I must go," said one young house slave to her former owner. "If I stay here I'll never know I am free."[118] This woman knew that living conditions might well be worse in the contraband camps or laboring on the plantations for the Union's benefit. But the greater goal of experiencing true freedom was worth the risk.

Indeed, under the circumstances, even death seemed a small price to pay. One Mississippi slave, known only as Cindy, left her home plantation with her husband Si when the Yankees came near. Unfortunately, the trip toward the Union lines proved too much for her. Already old and rather feeble, she did not survive the journey. Some time later, the couple's former master caught up with Si and demanded to know why he had brought Cindy on the journey with him. After all, the master pointed out, Si must have known that the trip could kill his wife. "I couldn't help it, marster," Si replied. "You see, she died free."[119]

Notes

Chapter 1: Women on the Northern Home Front

1. Quoted in Sylvia G.L. Dannett, *Noble Women of the North,* New York: Thomas Yoseloff, 1959, p. 38.
2. Quoted in Mary Elizabeth Massey, *Bonnet Brigades.* New York. Knopf, 1966, p. 30.
3. Agatha Young, *The Women and the Crisis.* New York: McDowell, Oblensky, 1959, p. 71.
4. Quoted in Elizabeth D. Leonard, *Yankee Women: Gender Battles in the Civil War.* New York: W. W. Norton, 1994, p. 54.
5. Quoted in Dannett, *Noble Women of the North,* p. 53.
6. Quoted in Leonard, *Yankee Women,* p. 102.
7. Quoted in Young, *The Women and the Crisis,* p. 31.
8. Quoted in Judith Ann Giesberg, *Civil War Sisterhood.* Boston: Northeastern University Press, 2000, p. 39.
9. Quoted in Frank Moore, *Women of the War.* Hartford, CT: S.S. Scranton, 1866, p. 371.
10. Quoted in Massey, *Bonnet Brigades,* p. 176.
11. Quoted in Giesberg, *Civil War Sisterhood,* p. 71.
12. Quoted in Willard A. Heaps and Porter W. Heaps, *The Singing Sixties.* Norman: University of Oklahoma Press, 1960, p. 95.
13. Quoted in Massey, *Bonnet Brigades,* p. 207.
14. Quoted in Leonard, *Yankee Women,* p. xviii.
15. Quoted in Giesberg, *Civil War Sisterhood,* p. 16.
16. Quoted in Leonard, *Yankee Women,* p. xiii.
17. Quoted in Heaps and Heaps, *The Singing Sixties,* p. 225.
18. Quoted in Massey, *Bonnet Brigades,* p. 216.
19. Quoted in Moore, *Women of the War,* p. 541.
20. Quoted in Leonard, *Yankee Women,* p. xiv.

Chapter 2: Women on the Southern Home Front

21. Quoted in Massey, *Bonnet Brigades,* p. 241.
22. Quoted in Massey, *Bonnet Brigades,* p. xiii.
23. Quoted in George C. Rable, *Civil Wars: Women and the Crisis of Southern Nationalism.* Urbana:

University of Illinois Press, 1989, p. 50.

24. Quoted in Drew Gilpin Faust, *Mothers of Invention.* Chapel Hill: University of North Carolina Press, 1996, p. 16.

25. Quoted in Faust, *Mothers of Invention,* p. 13.

26. Quoted in Mary Boykin Chesnut, *A Diary from Dixie.* Gloucester, MA: Peter Smith, 1961, p. 178.

27. Quoted in Walter Sullivan, *The War the Women Lived.* Nashville: J.S. Sanders, 1995, p. 182.

28. Quoted in Faust, *Mothers of Invention,* p. 123.

29. Quoted in Faust, *Mothers of Invention,* p. 57.

30. Parthenia Antoinette Hague, *A Blockaded Family.* Boston: Houghton Mifflin, 1888, p. 153.

31. Chesnut, *A Diary from Dixie,* p. 38.

32. Quoted in Rable, *Civil Wars,* p. 92.

33. Hague, *A Blockaded Family*, p. 54.

34. Quoted in Rable, *Civil Wars,* p. 93.

35. Hague, *A Blockaded Family*, p. 102.

36. Quoted in Massey, *Bonnet Brigades,* p. 202.

37. Quoted in Rable, *Civil Wars,* p. 98.

38. Quoted in Massey, *Bonnet Brigades,* p. 209.

39. Quoted in Rable, *Civil Wars,* p. 109.

40. Quoted in Sullivan, *The War the Women Lived,* p. 103.

41. Quoted in Massey, *Bonnet Brigades,* p. 231.

42. Hague, *A Blockaded Family,* p. 145.

43. Quoted in Rable, *Civil Wars,* p. 186.

44. Quoted in Katharine M. Jones, *When Sherman Came: Southern Women and the 'Great March.'* Indianapolis: Bobbs-Merrill, 1964, p. 155.

45. Quoted in Sullivan, *The War the Women Lived,* p. 229.

46. Quoted in Jones, *When Sherman Came,* p. 255.

Chapter 3: Nurses

47. Quoted in Massey, *Bonnet Brigades,* p. 54.

48. Quoted in Faust, *Mothers of Invention,* p. 93.

49. Quoted in Massey, *Bonnet Brigades,* p. 51.

50. Quoted in Young, *The Women and the Crisis,* p. 98.

51. Quoted in Young, *The Women and the Crisis,* p. 45.

52. Quoted in Massey, *Bonnet Brigades,* p. 44.

53. Quoted in Massey, *Bonnet Brigades,* p. 51.

54. Quoted in Faust, *Mothers of Invention,* p. 93.

55. Quoted in Faust, *Mothers of Invention,* p. 106.

56. Quoted in Massey, *Bonnet Brigades,* following p. 164.

57. Quoted in Giesberg, *Civil War Sisterhood,* p. 126.

58. Quoted in Sullivan, *The War the Women Lived,* p. 149.

59. Quoted in Young, *The Women and the Crisis,* pp. 165–166.

60. Quoted in Faust, *Mothers of Invention,* p. 104.

61. Moore, *Women of the War,* p. 347.

62. Moore, *Women of the War,* p. 317.

63. Quoted in Young, *The Women and the Crisis,* p. 93.

64. Quoted in Faust, *Mothers of Invention,* p. 108.

65. Quoted in Leonard, *Yankee Women,* p. 47.

Chapter 4: Camp Women

66. Moore, *Women of the War,* p. 255.

67. Quoted in Moore, *Women of the War,* p. 256.

68. Quoted in Massey, *Bonnet Brigades,* p. 67.

69. Quoted in Richard Hall, *Patriots in Disguise.* New York: Paragon House, 1993, p. 17.

70. Quoted in Massey, *Bonnet Brigades,* p. 69.

71. Quoted in Massey, *Bonnet Brigades,* p. 68.

72. Young, *The Women and the Crisis,* p. 95.

73. Quoted in Lee Middleton, *Hearts of Fire.* Franklin, NC: Genealogy Publishing Service, 1993, p. 59.

74. Quoted in Elizabeth D. Leonard, *All the Daring of a Soldier.* New

York: W.W. Norton, 1999, p. 152.

75. Quoted in Massey, *Bonnet Brigades,* p. 85.

76. Quoted in Stephen Currie, *Music in the Civil War.* Cincinnati: Betterway Books, 1992, p. 43.

77. Quoted in Moore, *Women of the War,* p. 256.

78. Moore, *Women of the War,* p. 57.

79. Moore, *Women of the War,* p. 111.

80. Quoted in Leonard, *All the Daring of a Soldier,* p. 147.

Chapter 5: Women Spies, Militias, and Soldiers

81. Quoted in Faust, *Mothers of Invention,* p. 217.

82. Quoted in Massey, *Bonnet Brigades,* p. 92.

83. Quoted in Moore, *Women of the War,* p. 171.

84. Quoted in Leonard, *All the Daring of a Soldier,* pp. 53–54.

85. Faust, *Mothers of Invention,* p. 217.

86. Quoted in Leonard, *All the Daring of a Soldier,* p. 26.

87. Quoted in Mrs. Thaddeus Horton, "The Story of the Nancy Harts," *Ladies Home Journal,* November 1904, p. 14.

88. Quoted in Mrs. Forrest T. Morgan, "'Nancy Harts' of the Confederacy," *Confederate Veteran,* vol. 30, 1922, p. 466.

89. Quoted in Horton, "The Story of the Nancy Harts," p. 14.

90. Quoted in Hall, *Patriots in Disguise,* p. 23.

91. Quoted in Middleton, *Hearts of Fire,* p. 157.

92. Quoted in Lauren Cook Burgess, ed., *An Uncommon Soldier.* Pasadena, MD: Minerva Center, 1994, p. 18.

93. Quoted in Burgess, *An Uncommon Soldier,* p. 3.

94. Quoted in Leonard, *Yankee Women,* p. 205.

95. Quoted in Hall, *Patriots in Disguise,* p. 157.

96. Quoted in Burgess, *An Uncommon Soldier,* p. xii.

97. Quoted in Leonard, *All the Daring of a Soldier,* p. 213.

98. Quoted in Hall, *Patriots in Disguise,* p. 179.

99. Quoted in Leonard, *All the Daring of a Soldier,* p. 252.

100. Quoted in Burgess, *An Uncommon Soldier,* p. 9.

101. Quoted in Middleton, *Hearts of Fire,* p. 163.

102. Quoted in Burgess, *An Uncommon Soldier,* p. 28.

Chapter 6: African American Women

103. Quoted in Massey, *Bonnet Brigades,* p. 57.

104. Quoted in Leonard, *All the Daring of a Soldier,* p. 153.

105. Massey, *Bonnet Brigades,* p. 268.

106. Chesnut, *A Diary from Dixie,* p. 38.

107. Quoted in Noralee Frankel, *Break Those Chains at Last.* New York: Oxford University Press, 1996, p. 23.

108. Quoted in Noralee Frankel, *Freedom's Women.* Bloomington: Indiana University Press, 1999, p. 25.

109. Quoted in Rable, *Civil Wars,* p. 118.

110. Quoted in Frankel, *Break Those Chains at Last,* p. 21.

111. Quoted in James C. Cobb, *The Most Southern Place on Earth.* New York: Oxford University Press, 1992, p. 41.

112. Quoted in Esther Hill Hawks, *A Woman Doctor's Civil War,* ed. Gerald Schwartz. Columbia: University of South Carolina Press, 1984, p. 70.

113. Quoted in Frankel, *Break Those Chains at Last,* p. 22.

114. Quoted in Faust, *Mothers of Invention,* p. 57.

115. Quoted in Cobb, *The Most Southern Place on Earth,* p. 41.

116. Quoted in Frankel, *Freedom's Women,* p. 33.

117. Hawks, *A Woman Doctor's Civil War,* p. 155.

118. Quoted in Frankel, *Break Those Chains at Last,* p. 44.

119. Quoted in Frankel, *Freedom's Women,* p. 26.

For Further Reading

Susan Provost Belier, *Confederate Ladies of Richmond*. Brookfield, CT: Twenty-First Century Books, 1999. Discusses women of the Confederate capital city and how they perceived and experienced the war.

Timothy Levi Biel, *Life in the North During the Civil War*. San Diego: Lucent Books, 1997. Provides information about daily life and difficulties in the Northern states.

Jean F. Blashfield, *Women at the Front*. New York: Franklin Watts, 1997. Describes the activities of Civil War women and also examines the changing roles of women in society during and after the war.

Stephen Currie, *Life of a Slave on a Southern Plantation*. San Diego: Lucent Books, 2000. A useful source of background information on slavery as slaves experienced it at the beginning of the Civil War.

————, *Music in the Civil War*. Cincinnati: Betterway Books, 1992. Contains information about music and its social, cultural, and military uses in the war. It also includes chapters on music on the home front and music of the slaves.

Phyllis Raybin Emert, *Women in the Civil War*. Lowell, MA: Discovery Enterprises, 1995. Provides information and background about the Civil War.

Noralee Frankel, *Break Those Chains at Last*. New York: Oxford University Press, 1996. Covers the years from the Civil War to 1880 in African American history.

Douglas Savage, *Women in the Civil War*. Philadelphia: Chelsea House, 2000. Provides background, activities, and biographical information for famous women and for women in general.

Works Consulted

❦

Books

B.A. Botkin, ed., *Lay My Burden Down: A Folk History of Slavery.* Chicago: University of Chicago Press, 1945. Excerpts from the Slave Narrative Collection gathered in the 1930s, interviews with men and women who had been slaves.

Lauren Cook Burgess, ed., *An Uncommon Soldier.* Pasadena, MD: Minerva Center, 1994. The edited and annotated letters of Sarah Rosetta Wakeman, who disguised herself as a man and fought with the Union army.

Mary Boykin Chesnut, *A Diary from Dixie.* Gloucester, MA: Peter Smith, 1961. Chesnut was a Confederate slaveholder and the wife of a politician. Her diary is one of the most interesting accounts available of Southern life during the Civil War.

Andrew Carroll, ed., *War Letters: Correspondence from American Wars.* New York: Scribner, 2001. A collection of letters written by and to American soldiers from the Revolutionary War to the present.

Includes a chapter on Civil War correspondence.

James C. Cobb, *The Most Southern Place on Earth.* New York: Oxford University Press, 1992. A history of the Mississippi Delta region, including some information on slave women and their female owners.

Sylvia G.L. Dannett, *Noble Women of the North.* New York: Thomas Yoseloff, 1959. A compilation of writings by Union women about the war, with background material by the author.

Drew Gilpin Faust, *Mothers of Invention.* Chapel Hill: University of North Carolina Press, 1996. An excellent description of the world of slaveholding Southern women during the Civil War.

Noralee Frankel, *Freedom's Women.* Bloomington: Indiana University Press, 1999. Describes the lives of African American women in Mississippi during the Civil War and afterward.

Judith Ann Giesberg, *Civil War Sisterhood.* Boston: Northeastern University Press, 2000. A scholarly study of soldiers' aid societies and women's political roles during and after the Civil War.

Parthenia Antoinette Hague, *A Blockaded Family.* Boston: Houghton Mifflin, 1888. One of the most vivid accounts of daily life in the Civil War South.

Richard Hall, *Patriots in Disguise.* New York: Paragon House, 1993. Discusses women who served as soldiers in the Civil War and also includes information on women spies.

Cornelia Hancock, *Letters of a Civil War Nurse.* Lincoln: University of Nebraska Press, 1998. This is a young woman's letters about her nursing experience.

Esther Hill Hawks, *A Woman Doctor's Civil War.* Ed. Gerald Schwartz. Columbia: University of South Carolina Press, 1984. Hawks traveled to South Carolina and Florida during the war to work with newly freed slaves.

Willard A. Heaps and Porter W. Heaps, *The Singing Sixties.* Norman: University of Oklahoma Press, 1960. This book contains lyrics, commentary, and occasional melodies for dozens of Civil War songs.

Edward T. James, ed., *Notable American Women.* Cambridge, MA: Belknap Press, 1971. This three-volume biographical encyclopedia contains entries on Belle Boyd, Harriet Tubman, Clara Barton, and many other Civil War figures.

Katharine M. Jones, *When Sherman Came: Southern Women and the 'Great March.'* Indianapolis: Bobbs-Merrill, 1964. Eyewitness accounts and first-hand experiences of Sherman's March to the Sea as told by women.

Elizabeth D. Leonard, *All the Daring of a Soldier.* New York: W. W. Norton, 1999. A well-written and carefully researched study of the women who spied and soldiered during the Civil War.

———, *Yankee Women: Gender Battles in the Civil War.* New York: W. W. Norton, 1994. Describes the lives of three Northern women who played important roles in the war and a good deal of analysis about changes in traditional gender roles as well.

Mary Elizabeth Massey, *Bonnet Brigades.* New York: Knopf, 1966. A very useful book, if somewhat dated in tone; it provides information on women's roles and contributions on both sides of the conflict.

Lee Middleton, *Hearts of Fire.* Franklin, NC: Genealogy Publishing Service, 1993. Contains brief sketches of women spies, soldiers, nurses, and half soldiers. Some of the accounts are taken directly from earlier sources without much commentary and may or may not be historically accurate.

Frank Moore, *Women of the War.* Hartford, CT: S.S. Scranton, 1866. Brings together the stories of many Union women who played a role in the conflict. The book is written in a flowery and ornate nineteenth-century style, and the facts and quotes may not always be reliable.

George C. Rable, *Civil Wars: Women and the Crisis of Southern Nationalism.* Urbana: University of Illinois Press, 1989. A well-written and well-argued account of how Southern women reacted to the war and its hardships.

Philip Van Doren Stern, *Secret Missions of the Civil War.* Chicago: Rand McNally, 1959. A discussion of the work of male and female spies.

Walter Sullivan, *The War the Women Lived.* Nashville: J.S. Sanders, 1995. Excerpts from the letters and diaries of about twenty Southern women are provided in this book.

Agatha Young, *The Women and the Crisis.* New York: McDowell, Oblensky, 1959. Focuses primarily on the women of the North, especially the nurses and soldiers' aid workers, and sets the women's work and experiences against the broader context of the war.

Periodicals

Mrs. Thaddeus Horton, "The Story of the Nancy Harts," *Ladies Home Journal.* November 1904.

Mrs. Forrest T. Morgan, "'Nancy Harts' of the Confederacy," *Confederate Veteran,* vol. 30, 1922.

Linda Wheeler, "On the Homefront and in Battle: A Conference Addresses the Civil War." *Washington Post,* April 5, 2000.

Index

Picture Credits

Cover photo: © CORBIS
© Bettmann/CORBIS, 16, 19 (left),
  71 (left), 90, 93
© CORBIS, 10, 13, 21, 47, 68, 69, 72,
  85
Georgia State Library, 77
© Hulton/Archive by Getty Images, 19

(right), 28, 32, 37, 38, 44, 48, 52, 87
Library of Congress, 17, 23, 40, 64
© Medford Historical Society
  Collection/CORBIS, 25, 57, 61
National Archives, 71 (right)
State Archives of Michigan, 80 (both)
Yale University Library, 97

About the Author

Stephen Currie is the author of more than forty books, including, for Lucent Books, *Life of a Slave on a Southern Plantation, Women Inventors,* and *Life in the Trenches.* He has also published a number of magazine articles and curriculum materials. He is a great-great-grandson of Sally Bull, a corporal in the Nancy Harts during the Civil War. Currently he lives in New York State with his wife, Amity, and children, Irene and Nick.